The Living Witness

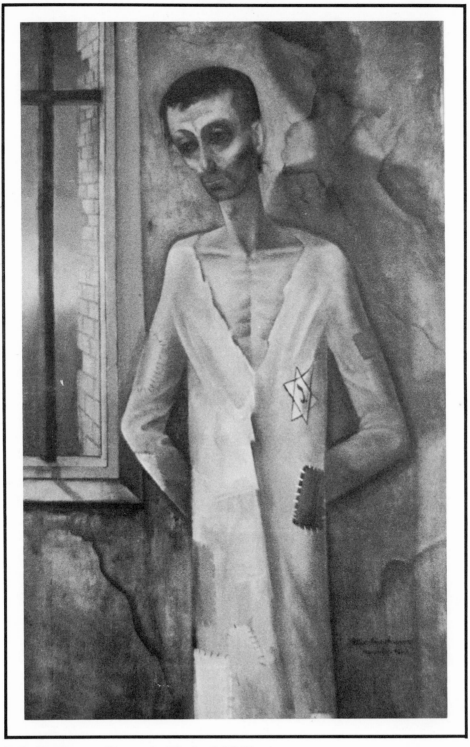

Felix Nussbaum   "Jew at the Window" (1942)
Painting, 26″ × 15″
Courtesy Osnabruck Museum, Germany

The Living Witness

Art in the Concentration Camps and Ghettos

Mary S. Costanza

THE FREE PRESS
A Division of Macmillan Publishing Co., Inc.
NEW YORK

Collier Macmillan Publishers
LONDON

The Free Press
A Division of Macmillan Publishing Co., Inc.
866 Third Avenue, New York, N. Y. 10022

Collier Macmillan Canada, Inc.

Library of Congress Catalog Card Number: 81-70859

Printed in the United States of America

printing number
1   2   3   4   5   6   7   8   9   10

Library of Congress Cataloging in Publication Data

Costanza, Mary S.
  The living witness.

  Includes index.
  1. Art, Jewish—Europe.   2. Holocaust, Jewish (1939-
1945), in art.   3. Holocaust, Jewish (1939-1945)—
Biography.   I. Title.
N7417.6.C67   741.94   81-70859
ISBN 0-02-906660-3   AACR2

To John

Tribute

I did not mean to stoke up the embers
  of painful recall, but of course,
  I did precisely that when I spoke
  to the artist-survivors of the
  Holocaust.

I could see that remembering crept
  through the black-out curtains
  of their minds, and tugged at
  them.

I could see that wisdom tempered any
  bitterness and that time had
  taken the edge off some pain.

I could see that the still-water experiences kept deep down for so
  long buoyed up and flowed out
  in reflection and conversation.

I could see that some had hoped to
  draw a shade on memory but it
  was not seal-proof.

These artist-survivors have merited
  some peace from pain, some relief from memory, some respite
  from their nightmares. Yet, that
  will not be.
The springs of the past seep back.
They will never forget; they will always remember.
They will carry with them all their
  lives this yoke that makes them a
  select society.
It will remain like an ever present nervous tic despite efforts to push it
  out of mind.
It is there forever,
  like the numbers imprinted on
  their arms, and the scars etched
  deeply on their hearts.

This book with great admiration and respect
is especially for:

Esther Lurie
Leo Haas
Osias Hofstatter
Halina Olomucki
Sara Gliksman Faitlovitz
Alfred Kantor
Alexander Bogen

for permitting me to invade their memories.

It was a privilege to be in their company for they gave me so much besides their time and their encouragement.
They gave me their trust and their friendship.
In moments of doubt, it was their faith in me that inspired me to complete this book as I promised.
For those who have died, and who are legend to me, now; and
For those whom I could not see and who are still among us, this is in commemoration of them.

I write this book with a pen dipped in love for my friends, the Artists of the Holocaust—
and their kin.

Mary Costanza

Contents

Leo Haas "March," Terezin Camp (1943)
Drawing, 18″ × 24″
Courtesy Leo Haas / Terezin Memorial Museum

During the early part of my imprisonment in Theresienstadt, I painted constantly. In spite of the fact that my suffering was great, and I was ill most of the time, I did not stop in my work. I made sketches and little paintings, and therefore my pictures are documentary. Some of these pictures which I have here, are originals which I drew while imprisoned in the "Small Fortress" and hid in the walls . . . These are all realistic paintings. But often, what I saw was much too dreadful to put on paper. My medium was too limited, and my paper too weak to bear all that I saw and felt.

Professor Leo Haas
Artist-survivor
East Berlin, 1979

foreword by Nora Levin

The torrent of documentation and literature on the Holocaust continues to assault the modern consciousness and shows no sign of stopping. Indeed, the outpouring of material has been especially profuse in recent years, streaming in from all directions. Some of it is plainly vulgar and offensive, worked up for cheap media exploitation and sensational effects. But serious minds are doing important work in the varied disciplines challenged by the subject. The Holocaust grips them as few human experiences in history have done, and continues to compel the interest and attention of growing circles of thoughtful men and women. Sooner or later, we come to realize that the events in Europe from 1933 to 1945 represent an axial change in human history, and the tenacious hold exerted by the history of that period reflects this understanding.

It has often been said that an abyss lies between the victims of Holocaust experiences and the rest of us. They have been described as having existed and died on another planet — "Planet Auschwitz," or *L'universe Concentrationnaire.* Serious minds have struggled to look into this abyss, to penetrate the universe of the victims, but they are frequently balked, because, as the author of *L'universe Concentrationnaire*, David Rousset, has said, "Normal men do not know that everything is possible. Even if the evidence forces their intelligence to admit it, their muscles do not believe it. . . . The concentrationees do know. . . . They are set apart from the rest of the world by an experience impossible to communicate." Not only did the Nazis devise new forms of human suffering and debasement, not only did they destroy old Western taboos against mass murder, they deliberately and systematically caused the disruption of every aspect of human beings that makes them human: the destruction of human bonds, of memory of a past life, of a sense of self, of the capacity to understand one's situation and to cope with it. The Nazi descent into "world without limit" made it possible to process human beings into matter, to create unpersons, to make the mass murder of Jews a civic virtue, to slaughter one and a half million children without guilt.

Our struggle to penetrate this·universe forces us, as Dr. Eva Fleischner, a Holocaust scholar, has said, "to touch bottom," to face hideous facts, peel away self-deceptions, search for gleams of humanity in that landscape of evil, confront our own natures and ask ultimate questions. No other chapter in human history has aroused so much self-searching or profound reflection. Our preoccupation with it not only measures our struggle to comprehend it but some deep agitated rebellion against the Nazi inversion of human values. The post-Holocaust world is a radically altered reality; familiar constraints and inhibitions were violated. Once shattered, can they ever be restored? Can the human image of man ever be recovered from the inhumanity of this century which, as André Malraux has said, killed man? Can we relearn the once human pain at mortal suffering? Our alienation from the old belief in humanity has become so great, yet, paradoxically, our hunger for it so strong, that we have invented a new type of specialist—the "humanist"—an "expert" who may somehow lead us toward a restored humanity we cannot find ourselves.

One may ask if writers and artists have been able to create imaginative works of the Holocaust that achieve the life-enhancing, cathartic transcendence we used to find in art. Critics do not think so. For a time, silence overwhelmed many writers who pondered the Holocaust, who sought a new language to describe it and new forms that would defy its meaninglessness. "The world of Auschwitz," George Steiner once believed, "lies outside speech as it lies outside reason." Others believed that writing poetry after Auschwitz would be "barbaric." But the silence has been broken and a "literature of atrocity" has appeared. The most searing works—and probably the most lasting—have been written by those on the other side of the abyss: Paul Celan, Oscar Pincus, Nelly

Sachs, André Schwartz-Bart, Elie Wiesel, Jerzy Kosinski. Their works are a new genre in the history of literature, yet there is no single climactic literary masterwork of the Holocaust. The excesses of that reality exceed the power of literature and art to render it, perhaps forever.

In the end, we go back to the massive documentation of the witnesses themselves for the most authentic sources of life and death in the Nazi subworld, to the hundreds of obsessed men and women who kept diaries, notebooks, and coded scraps which they buried or smuggled to friendly hands. More than death, they feared that the world would never know what they were enduring and, worse, that they would not be believed. But the need to record and bear witness was as elemental as hunger and worth risking life for. These messages, from the calmly detached to the terror-crazed, tell us more about the unspeakable hells of the Holocaust than any body of creative literature. Formless, unedited, sometimes incoherent, these are the raw transcripts of experiences as they were lived, jabbing us with an intensity and immediacy that cannot and should not be relieved or consoled by transcendence. We have to feel the crushing pain, the desolation, the ghastliness.

Similarly, although we have a body of postwar art dealing with Holocaust themes by artists such as Ben Shahn, Rico Lebrun, Mauricio Lasansky, and Audrey Flack, they are of a different order and time from the drawings and sketches made by artists in the ghettos and camps. These works, like the diaries and notebooks, are literal transcripts of life as it was, with the added power of visual imagery. The suffering depicted is incapable of transfiguration. It is there in hunger-haunted faces, in heaps of skeletons denied the dignity of burial, in eyes that stare out of deep sockets with despair and abandonment.

We now have hundreds of diaries and extensive personal testimony in writing, much of which has been published in the last five or ten years, but until now, with the publication of Mary Costanza's book, there have been few works dealing with art produced by artist-witnesses of the Holocaust. There have been some reproductions in brochures and museum catalogs and occasional exhibits, and a few books, but Mrs. Costanza's book is the first systematic effort by a practical artist to reproduce and record the work of Holocaust artists, which she found in collections in Israel, Europe, and the United States. Hundreds of hitherto unknown works and their creators are now revealed to us, and the visual documentation is as astonishing as the written material. That any art could have been created under the conditions of Nazi terror and atrocity is, as in the case of the secret diarists, yet another measure of the indomitable will of many of the marked victims. With terrible urgency, they sketched and drew on flour bags, shreds of paper, the tiny margins of stamps, and potato sacks. Zoran Music exclaimed, "Tomorrow may be too late. . . . Life and death depended on these sheets." Alfred Kantor, an eighteen-year-old art student in the ghetto of Terezin and later in Auschwitz, said he sketched secretly out of a "deep instinct of self-preservation [which] undoubtedly helped me to deny the unimaginable horrors of that time. By taking on the role of an 'observer' I could at least for a few moments detach myself from what was going on at Auschwitz and was therefore better able to hold together the threads of sanity. In Auschwitz I felt obsessed. . . . I began to observe everything with an eye towards capturing it on paper: the searching for lice, the women carrying soup in heavy barrels, the incredibly eerie feeling of Auschwitz at night with its strange lights and . . . the glow of flames from the crematorium."

Some of the artists represented were already well known at the time of their persecution: Leo Haas, Felix Nussbaum, Otto Freundlich, Karl Schweisig, and Roman Kramztyk, among others. A number were identified with particular art movements or schools, such as Dada, German Expressionism, Surrealism, and Abstractionism. Alfred Kantor, Dinah Gottliebova, Peter Kien, and Adolf Aussenberg were among the budding students. Some began drawing in the camps and ghettos. All of Europe nourished these artists: Germany, Holland, France, Poland, Italy, Czechoslovakia. The grotesque subworld of the Nazis provided them with their last landscapes and settings. Many who worked for the Nazis in the camps and ghettos making graphs, charts, counterfeit money, and copies of plundered masterpieces, did their real work in secret at great peril, and died for it. Few of the artists survived, but with the publication of Mrs. Costanza's book, the testimony of their works will.

The Living Witness is not only a path-breaking work which will provide the basis for future research on Holocaust art, but it is that rare fusion of work and creator. This vast canvas of human suffering has found its most fitting author, for although Mrs. Costanza herself is not a survivor, she has lived intensely with Holocaust experiences since the end of World War II, and has devoted much of her own art, including paintings, drawings, and lithographs, to the Holocaust, particularly to the suffering of women and children. *The Living Witness* is a natural outgrowth of her own preoccupation with the Holocaust. From her own work, she was drawn to the work of artists of that time. Lectures and then formal courses—probably the first anywhere—at Gratz College developed into the present book.

Infinite compassion and sorrow fill this book; an overpowering sense of loss brims over every line. Critical analysis of the artists' works would be rudely out of place and offensive, yet Mrs. Costanza comments with great sensitivity. What can compare with Terezin and Gurs and Auschwitz? The works reproduced and described cannot be pressed into schools of art, or styles. They stand apart, singular and terrible, like the written testimony of the Holocaust. These drawings proclaim the individual spirit struggling against the massed deaths. We see the individual's vision—spectral and desolating—but a pair of human eyes and human hands are at work in a human activity, and they beseech us to suffer with them. Suffering is also human. Holocaust art cannot be transfigured into anything other than suffering. This is the inescapable reality which no writer or artist can transcend, and this is the truth Mary Costanza wishes us to experience. Artists of the Holocaust can have no more tender or sensitive steward of their legacy.

Karel Fleischmann   Terezin (1942)
Charcoal drawing, 18″ × 24″
Courtesy Prague State Jewish Museum

*One of us
   will teach these children how to sing again,
   to write on paper with a pencil,
   to do sums and multiply,
   One of us
   is sure to survive.*

Karel Fleischmann
Terezin, 1942

Preface

There has been no period in recorded history when witnesses left such a vast number of visual documents about their experiences of terror as did the artists incarcerated in the concentration and death camps of Europe. They refused to allow the truth to be buried in that abyss of the untold.

Out of that *Schlactfeld*—the vast slaughter field of Europe—and out of the ashes of the camps have arisen, like an indestructible Phoenix, an enormous number of art works. Works keep surfacing! There are hundreds in existence, spread out all over the globe, some as far away from the scene of the crime as Australia.[1] In all instances the subject matter is the same: suffering, brutality, hunger, degradation, and murder. Countless artists bear testimony to these experiences. This creative activity went on feverishly throughout the entire concentration camp system, even in some of the death camps such as Auschwitz. The surge of energy spent by these artists, often to their own detriment, is a marvel in itself. This was the artists' "rage against the dying of the light."

I can almost say that I understand the motives of the artists' clandestine and bold productivity. They feared that the widespread and wanton destruction by the Nazis would never come to light, that few would know or tell about it.[2] They were most clairvoyant about this fear; only recently have writers begun to include this chapter of the Holocaust history. Many Nazis have found comfortable berths for themselves in every part of the world: the United States, Europe, South America, Africa.[3] Owing to the dedicated efforts of people like Simon Wiesenthal, the husband-wife team of Beate and Serge Klarsfeld of France, and Reinhard Strecker of Germany, author of the book, *Dr. Hans Globke,*[4] some of these Nazis have been found and exposed. It is only recently, too, that articles such as Umberto Giovane's *Dibattiti Dopo Holocaust* have appeared, often naming those criminals at large.[5] As the Nazis are ferreted out, camps whose existence was previously unknown to the public are unearthed, such as La Risiera di San Sabba in Trieste, referred to as the Auschwitz of Italy, which in 1944 became an extermination center.[6]

I have always empathized with the artists in the camps and, I believe, I share with them their purpose. One of these artists, Alexander Bogen, apologizing for his poor English, eloquently expressed the purpose, corroborated by all the artist-survivors with whom I have been in touch:

> I asked myself why I was drawing, when I was fighting day and night. This is something similar to biological continuity. Every man, every people, is interested to continue his people, his family, to bring his creative children for the future—to leave this one thing. Another motivation was to bring information to the so-named free world about the actions, the cruel, cruel actions of the Germans—some documentation. To tell about this to a world that was uninformed. . . . To be creative in the situation of the Holocaust, this is also a protest. Each man when he is standing face to face with cruel danger, with death, reacts in his way. The artist reacts with his means. This is his protest! This is my means! He reacts in an artistic way. This is his weapon. He must leave his mark as a *mensch* on mankind. This, it shows that the Germans could not break his spirit.

I first learned about art work produced in the concentration camps when I read Nora Levin's book *The Holocaust: The Destruction of European Jewry.* In the chapter on Terezin she described activity in the arts which included painting and drawing. I found this mind boggling. (As an artist, I never work when I am under stress or not at peace with myself.) Although the core of much of my own work is the depiction of human suffering, it is no great task to make these commentaries from the vantage point and the solitude of a comfortable studio. But these artists were caught up in that maelstrom, experiencing all the agony and pain. To me this was unfathomable, and in reflection, even after all this time, it seems utterly miraculous.

The thought had crossed my mind to pursue this compelling study, but the catalyst was Nora Levin, whose suggestion that I prepare a syllabus for presentation to Gratz College[7] for possible inclusion in their program charted my course on this star.

At the outset I realized there was no central source to which I could go for information. In fact, many scholars whom I approached had never heard of such a thing as art work produced in the camps. My initial plan had been to spend a summer preparing a program for the Gratz course, which had been accepted. Instead, my work continues to this day. My research actually began over four years ago with the writing of letters—hundreds of letters—to friends involved in Holocaust studies, authors, historians, survivors, artists, and government officials. I contacted museums, archives, universities, and documentation centers throughout the United States, Europe, and Israel.

I took addresses from footnotes in books, and risked writing to incomplete addresses I found or heard about in conversation. I scanned publications, periodicals, and newspapers. In truth, I received responses from almost everyone to whom I wrote. The latest response has come from Moscow. As answers to my queries poured in from all over the world, the arrival of the mail became the most important time of day for me. (The envelopes and wrappings themselves are a philatelist's delight.) A virtual avalanche of material in the form of individually typewritten pages, actual documents, pamphlets, catalogs, magazines, newspaper clippings, small books, and sizable tomes was sent to me. At times even original works were offered. If my letters reached a destination no longer in existence, they came back to me from as far away as Germany, France, Italy, and Czechoslovakia. If those I addressed had no information, my letters were passed on to others who had. The willingness to help me was inspirational, and the excitement at the discovery of new material mixed with a tempering melancholy were the paradoxical emotions that enveloped me throughout this entire course of research.

It soon became apparent that the unusual situation would be the norm and the unique circumstance prevail in this research.

So much material and so many gifts have fallen into my hands from both solicited and unsolicited sources that space permits only the recounting of a few of these coincidences.

It is my habit to go along the rows of books on library shelves in the Holocaust section looking for new material. This is how I came across *Dachau: The Harrowing of Hell.* What had caught my eye at first about this particular book were the drawings in it. All of them were legibly signed: "Zoran Music, 1945, Dachau." The foreword explained that the artist was presumed dead. In my correspondence with Dr. Marcus Smith, the author, he recalled that after the army unit in which he was a medical officer had liberated Dachau, a prisoner had given him the drawings in gratitude. Meanwhile, I was corresponding with an artist-survivor in Copenhagen, Olly Ritterband, whose Holocaust art work I had seen on a postcard put out by the Nationalmuseet in Denmark. Upon her suggestion I wrote to the director of the Nationalmuseet. He sent me a catalog of the museum's most recent exhibit on Holocaust art with the explanation that this was all that was available at the time. The work was by the artist, Zoran Music, who had been incarcerated in Dachau and was now living in Venice and Paris. It took one year, and a trip to the Vatican Museum, where I was given Music's correct address, before I finally got in touch with him, and he, ultimately, with Dr. Smith. Zoran Music had no idea that some of his work had reached the United States.

After a lecture in which I expressed frustration over not being able to contact certain artists, such as Charlotte Buresova, while I was in Prague, a woman who knew Buresova personally and visited her each time she went to Prague offered to help me contact her. This woman was herself a survivor who had worked in Terezin's craft workshop making artificial flowers during her imprisonment. That night I got Charlotte Buresova's address in Prague from a woman in New Jersey, and the artist has become another one of my friends on paper.

Other unsolicited gifts fell into my hands. A television appearance brought a phone call from a woman survivor who introduced me to one of the great finds of this research: sixty-one pieces of art by her brother, Peter Loewenstein. That phone call also reunited her with a former Czech friend whom I had come to know, the artist Alfred Kantor. Alfred Kantor was, along with Peter Loewenstein, in that first contingent of Jews sent to Terezin. Because Alfred Kantor's name is listed as one of the deceased Jews on the Memorial Tablet in the Pincas Synagogue in Prague, she had presumed him dead. (For years Alfred Kantor has been trying unsuccessfully to get his name removed from that list.) Not only were they reunited but they discovered that they were virtually neighbors.

Somewhere along the line I had heard that Leo Haas, one of the four artists who had been punished when some of his secret art work was found in Terezin, was still alive and living somewhere in East Germany. Repeated attempts to locate him were fruitless until one day I was bemoaning this fact to a colleague, Dr. Franklin Littell. Dr. Littell had a brother who was chief of the U.S. Staff of the International Communication Agency in Berlin, and within a month Leo Haas and I were writing to each other.

As others heard about this heretofore unknown aspect of Holocaust history, requests for data came to me from all over the world. Often responses to my own inquiries were accompanied by requests for any information I might have accumulated, and a kind of data exchange developed. I had by this time a voluminous amount of material and found myself sending out bits and pieces of it. As I realized the need for a central source, the idea for the book materialized.

My European and Israeli contacts made me quite aware that my book could not be completed if I did not see the material first hand. Invited to visit them, my husband, John, and I planned an itinerary.

Each leg of the journey was as diverse as each situation that confronted us was unique, but in each place we found something that helped fill in the gaps of this history, and the picture of this activity crystallized. I found two or three pieces in the Vatican's contemporary archives, where I spent the better part of a day, saw the larger collections in Israel and Czechoslovakia, and spent a memorable few days with Leo Haas in East and West Berlin.

Israel was rich with information. This is where I met most of the artist-survivors who were the most informative, helpful, and generous of all. Yad Vashem Memorial Museum is an experience in itself. Opening its archives to me, I was provided with full assistance of the staff and spent three productive days there, studying, photographing, and getting data I needed.

I had never been to a camp before Terezin. After we met the director and the staff, an elderly woman who spoke English fluently was assigned to act as our guide. We saw the dreaded fortress in its entirety: the solitary confinement cells, including the one in which Leo Haas had been imprisoned; the blocks; the hospital with its pitifully small rusted cots; the shooting wall; the gallows; the place from which the sole escapee from the fortress had stolen away; the web of underground passages; the building where the SS were billeted (now the administrative offices); and finally, across the courtyard, down a birch-lined path to the former SS headquarters, which now housed the archives and the finest museum of Holocaust art and artifacts that I have ever seen. The exhibit of works by Leo Haas, Otto Ungar, Bedrich Fritta, Petr Kien, and so many more was beautifully mounted, handsomely displayed, and the entire museum space exquisitely designed. Everything was professionally done and I was impressed by the great care given to the collection. If I recall correctly, even the temperature was regulated for the preservation of the works — many of which were in a fragile state.

This study has not involved just the discovery and collection of data. There were some rather poignant human encounters. Some survivors found friends they thought had perished. Some artists discovered that works they thought had been destroyed had in fact been salvaged. All whose lives we touched showed concern about and interest in my work. All expressed the feeling that the only hope for the future would be the dissemination of information about what had happened in Europe. These experiences confirmed our belief that if people meet on a one-to-one basis, ideological barriers and prejudices can be overcome. As we brush each others' lives with courtesy and respect for the hosts in whose lands we are guests, the encounters can be enriching and friends can be made. These meetings more importantly point out our similarities rather than our differences, which in the end are perhaps the only way to avert such a tragedy as a Holocaust. This is what we learned, John and I, in the collation of material for this book.[8]

Acknowledgments

That I was able to write this book is due entirely to the many who contributed generously of their time, information, and experiences. All the material—from the tiniest news clipping to the collections in the museums and archives—was instrumental in the putting together of this gigantic puzzle. The enthusiastic support, cooperation, and encouragement induced me to dare to write this book. To many people and institutions I owe more than I can ever say:

Professor Nora Levin, author, historian, and teacher, spent many hours editing my manuscript, provided me with a continuous supply of material from her own sources and research, and always gave me cherished friendship and valuable advice; Professor Alice Eckardt of the Religious Studies Department of Lehigh University was among the first to answer my requests for information, as was Robert St. John, author, lecturer, and expert on the Middle East, who sent me many articles; Dr. Marcus Smith, medical doctor and author, generously shared his Zoran Music drawings and his knowledge with me; Stella Gabuzda, linguist and resource librarian at Ludington Library in my home town, patiently spent many hours of her own time translating Czech, Danish, and other documents for me.

Reinhard Strecker, author, teacher at Goethe Institute in West Berlin, and our gracious host in Germany, was my liaison and interpreter in my conversations with Leo Haas, and loaned me volumes of literature pertinent to my subject. The honorable Gian Carlo Riccio, consul general of Italy in Philadelphia, arranged a meeting with Dr. Carlo Pietrangeli, director of the Vatican Mu-

xxiii

seum in Rome, and Dr. Mario Ferrazza, curator of the contemporary collection, both of whom permitted me to see the archives and exhibits. Kitty Moore, my sensitive and perceptive editor at the Free Press, gave me advice and direction that helped make my first encounter with the publishing world a most positive experience.

The debt I owe the people in Czechoslovakia is inestimable. Director Vaclav Novak and Dr. Miroslav Kryl of the Terezin Memorial Museum gave me access to their archives, permitted me to photograph the material there, and assigned to me their entire curatorial staff, including: historian and our interpreter, Dr. George Maleninsky; the chief archivist, Dr. Jaroslava Bezdekova; the assistant archivist, Michaela Feixova; apprentice Jan Toman; and our fortress guide, Madam Nina Nachmannova. To these people my humble thanks and affection for all their time, thoughtfulness, and hospitality.

Director Miroslav Jaros of the Prague State Jewish Museum made it possible to work and photograph the work in that unusual collection of Holocaust material and also put his staff at my disposal: young chief archivist, Arno Panik, and interpreter, Dr. Jirina Seinova.

Dr. Gideon Hausner and Dr. Yitzak Arad of the Yad Vashem Memorial Museum permitted me to use the material in that archive, and allowed me the assistance of their staff, especially Ilana Guri, archivist.

I owe many thanks to these individuals and institutions who provided material and permission for its use in this book:

Gerda Korngold, sister of Peter Loewenstein; the Reverend Donald Clifford, O.J. (the clipping he sent from abroad opened up a whole new area in my research); Dr. Franklin Littell and Dr. Wallace Littell helped me to locate Leo Haas; Thomas Fritta Haas of Germany, son of Bedrich Fritta and adopted son of Leo Haas; Simon Wiesenthal of the Documentation Center in Vienna; British author Madelaine Duke; and Janina Jaworska of Poland, who sent me her excellent and informative book *Nie Wsyzytek Umre*; Dr. Henryk Swiebocki of the Auschwitz Memorial Museum, who generously supplied much of the literature and documents about the Auschwitz Memorial Museum, and Dr. Kazimierz Smolen, also of the Memorial; Professor Paul M. G. Levy, president of the National Memorial of Fort Breendonk, Belgium, supplied me with important data, especially on Jacques Ochs; Dr. Manfred Meinz, director of the Kulturgeschichtliches Museum, Osnabruck, sent me the excellent material on Felix Nussbaum; Dr. Hans Biereigel of the Nationale Mahn und Gedenkstatte, Sachsenhausen, sent photographs and literature from that collection; Dr. M. Trostorff, Director of the Nationale Mahn und Gedenkstatte, Buchenwald, sent me many books; Professor Maurycy Horn, director of the Jewish Historical Institute in Warsaw, and Dr. Zigmunt Hoffman, also of the Institute; Jergen H. Barfod, director of the Nationalmuseet in Denmark, and Dr. Pieter Koepplin, director of the Kunstmuseum in Basel, Switzerland, sent me information about Zoran Music; Gita Johnson of the Contemporary History and Wiener Library and Paul Shaw of the Board of Deputies of British Jews, London; Director Janina Grabowska of the Stuttof Museum, Poland; Claudine Cohen-Naar of the Centre de Documentation Juive Contemporaine, Paris, supplied material on Violette Le Coq and Liesel Felsenthal; Director Andrzek Budzynski of the Pawiak Memorial Museum in Poland; Direktorin Dr. Haak, Nationale Mahn and Gedenkstatte, Ravensbruck; Director Damian Tomczyk of the Museum of Martyrology in Lambinowice; Ilona Fisher of the Israel Museum; Dorit Yif'at of the Tel Aviv Museum; Miriam Novitch of the Biet Lohamei Haghetaot, Israel; Dr. O. Hacker of the Department of the Interior in Vienna, Austria, who put me in touch with the Atelier Fuhrherr who handles the Mauthausen Camp Collection; and the Leo Baeck Institute, New York.

I would like to thank the Memorial Foundation for Jewish Culture, which awarded me a small grant that paid for my traveling expenses; Rosalie Kiely, my good-natured typist; my students at Gratz College, especially Gertrude Field, who were the best supporters and clipping service one could ever want; and, of course, my gratitude to the artists-survivors with whom I spoke and whom I interviewed, and to those artist-survivors I have come to know through correspondence: Charlotte Buresova and Helga Weissova-Hoskova of Prague; Liesel Felsenthal-Basnitzki of Israel; Dinah Gottliebova-Babbitt of the United States; and Zoran Music of Italy.

Finally, special thanks to my family, who shared so much with me: Nina, my daughter, covered those conferences I could not attend in New York, and helped with some of the editing; Jon, my son, and his wife, Lori, were supportive with candid and helpful suggestions, and were always willing to help in any way; and above all my husband, John, photographer, designer, recorder, and fellow traveler, who spent many hours away from his own work to help me make this book a reality.

The Living Witness

Alfred Kantor "Distribution of the Soup," Schwarzheide Camp (1944)
Pen and ink drawing, 3½" × 2¼"
Courtesy Alfred Kantor

Terezin . . . was an unusual place, and of all the experiences of my life I find those the most difficult to describe. . . . In Auschwitz I felt obsessed, driven in fact by the overwhelming desire to put down every detail of this unfathomable place. I began to observe everything with an eye towards capturing it on paper: At first I began to memorize scenes of the day's activity and then draw them at night in the barracks when no one was looking. It would have been too dangerous to draw in the open during the day while on a work brigade. . . . In Schwarzheide . . . my only opportunity to draw came at night in the barracks. I sketched, and then destroyed the drawings but committed them to memory. Once drawn, these scenes could never be erased from my mind.

Alfred Kantor
Artist-survivor
Irvington, New York, 1978

The Nightmare in the Language of Symbols:

A Place for Artists

Out of the trauma of the Holocaust era arose an awesome phenomenon. A body of artwork was produced and eventually salvaged to become a part of the art of the twentieth century. The artwork augments the mounting literature on the Holocaust, supplementing the written documents to make the incredible credible, as both artistic, humanistic statements and historical documents. The guide book to the Auschwitz Memorial Museum states, regarding the exhibits now housed in Block 6, Room 5; "Such terrible sights are presented by painters, men and women, who were prisoners themselves. Faithfully rendered, these scenes of camp existence have the value of document and evidence, they are a terrible accusation of the Nazi criminals."[1] This art is as vital as the most scholarly work of the historians, writers, survivors, and the many documents and photographs left by the maniacal record keepers themselves, the Nazis, and the liberation forces.[2] Now we have the catastrophe in unquestionable visual terms.

Many authors, among them Elie Wiesel, claim there are no words in any language that can describe this chapter in the history of man. Nora Levin, noted historian, says, "comprehensibility may never be possible."[3] Avraham Golub-Tory, member of the "Matzok" (the underground) and of the *Eltestenrat* (the Jewish council) of the Kovno Ghetto, writes: "The written word was not enough. Without graphic representations, the true sorrow of life struggling under the Nazi domination could not be fully documented."[4] Leon

Delarbre, artist-prisoner in Auschwitz, Buchenwald, Bergen-Belsen, and Dora, writes in the foreword to a compilation of his drawings published after the liberation, "This book has no title because one cannot find a word to express what with the European Jews happened."[5]

Language of the Familiar

When words and imaginations fail, the visual image can fill the hiatus, and give us a new source of knowledge. As Dr. Burton Wasserman, artist, art historian, and author, writes: "No matter how silent a work of art may seem to be, it has an amazing capacity for talking to us, if we pay attention to what it has to say in the language of design."[6]

To penetrate the contents of a book one must open it and then be able to read the language in which it is written. The pictorial image eliminates the language barrier. The only necessary prerequisites for understanding the visual message are the gift of sight and a receptive mind. This is especially true of the imagery that uses recognizable symbols. With visual symbols, the contact is immediate, direct, and the image is retained. The reknowned art historian, Sir Kenneth Clark, said: "The truths which Art has been able to communicate have been a kind which could not have been put in any other way. They have been ultimate truths, stated symbolically."[7]

The forms of a child, a woman, a man, a tree, or a bird are forms so universal that even the most primitive peoples can understand the signs. There is no mystery to probe, no ambiguity in the meaning of these modern-day hieroglyphics. The symbols do not vary from culture to culture. An outstanding artist of our time, Leonard Baskin, states, "The human figure is the image of all men and of one man. It contains all and can express all."

By composing the elements of design—line, form, color—singly or in any combination, the artist can make the symbols say certain

Starved
(How long did he suffer, until death redeemed him?)

Zoran Music Dachau Camp (1945)
Pencil drawing, 7½″ × 11″
Courtesy Dr. Marcus Smith

Photograph taken
during liberation by
Army Sergeant
Joseph M. Stellag,
1st Armored Division,
423 F.A. Battalion,
Bty "B", Third Army
Dachau Camp (1945)
Collection of the author

Karol Konieczny   "Leichenberg," Buchenwald Camp (1945)
Watercolor, 7″ × 5″
Courtesy Buchenwald Memorial Museum

Photograph taken
during liberation by
Army Sergeant
Joseph M. Stellag,
1st Armored Division,
423 F.A. Battalion,
Bty "B", Third Army
Dachau Camp (1945)
Collection of the author

Leon Delarbre   Dora (Buchenwald) Camp (1945)
Charcoal drawing, 6 " × 7½ "
Courtesy Hans Biereigel, Sachsenhausen Memorial Museum

things. They can be arranged, juxtaposed, designed in such a way that they can evoke any emotion, depict any situation, and transmit any message that the skillful artist wishes to convey. We can sense pain and fear as a child is torn from the arms of its mother; horror at witnessing a hanging, a beating, a selection; the pangs of hunger at the sight of emaciated shadows grappling for food. A turn of line, a shape of form, a shade of color can make all the difference in the presentation of any situation from human pathos to human joy to the abstract interplay of line, color, and/or form. An artist creates the mood and sets the stage for the layman's reaction and response. Otto Freundlich, a victim of the Nazis, whose paintings and sculptures they destroyed, and who was himself murdered in Maidanek death camp, stated: "In order to link the painting and the viewer an action is necessary. . . . It is the artist who creates in a painting a set of pictorial actions, the synthesis of which the viewer seeks."[8]

It is significant therefore that artists of the concentration camps who wanted to expose the inhuman conditions around them used the language of the familiar. This is common among the humanist artists, for whom a major concern is communication. Ben Shahn relates about another tragedy: "I now began to devise symbols of an almost abstract nature, to work in terms of such symbols. Then I rejected that approach too. For in the abstracting of an idea one may lose the very intimate humanity. And this deep and common tragedy was above all things human."[9] The artists of the camps were fully aware of the need to retain that intimacy with humanity in order to communicate. Many who were working in more contemporary directions prior to their incarceration resorted to more familiar art language while imprisoned.

The artists of the camps sketched on any surface they could find and used the found objects of their camp milieu. Herbert Read, distinguished art historian claims: "An artist will use the materials placed in his hands by the circumstances of his time; at one period he will scratch on the walls of his cave, at another he will build or decorate a temple or a cathedral, at another he will paint on canvas."[10] Like the Sabatino Rudio spires of Watts,[11] created in the midst of poverty and scorn, and with the found objects in the backyard of his own shanty, the camp artists, impoverished and alone, built their own spiral of monuments. These monuments, however, do not pierce the sky, they pierce the conscience. When the artists could not find any surface, they used the walls of their cells. There

Leo Haas Terezin Camp
Litho pencil drawing, 9″ × 12″
Courtesy Terezin Memorial Museum

Ota Matousek Flossenburg Camp (1943–1945)
Wash drawing
Courtesy Sachsenhausen Memorial Museum

are walls in cells in Fort Breendonk, the notorious prison in Belgium, upon which prisoners scratched drawings. An unknown artist left his mark at the Auschwitz-Birkenau barrack, B 1b. On the whitewashed ceiling of the prison is a mural, done in black and white, of the prisoners—the penal squad—working on the canal called "Konigsgraben" (the royal ditch). "Barely two kilometers long and built at the cost of three thousand lives, it would be easy to compute the numbers of prisoners who perished to complete one meter of the ditch." The drawing is amazingly well preserved at the Auschwitz site.[12]

A New Era in Humanistic Art

I will be referring to the work done in secret by artists in the camps as "humanistic art." There are diverse opinions and complex explanations as to the meaning and functions of art in general, and of humanistic art as well. Simply put, humanistic art depicts the ills and injustices in society as the artist sees them with the hope and expectation that some action by the powers that be will taken to rectify the malady. The artwork can be political, such as in the works of Daumier, Grosz, Rivera, Goya, Pissarro; social, as in the powerful drawings and graphics of Kathe Kollwitz, Baskin, Gropper, Orozco; religious, as in the works of Cranach, Holbein, Roualt, and even Michelangelo. This art always champions the cause of the underdog.[13] Confusing the issue, perhaps, is that this type of art has borne many labels: social protest, stream of consciousness, social conscious art, social commentary, and others. Whatever the label, the works of the artists of the camps are examples of humanistic art in its most meaningful and powerful context.

Since I will be making reference to the artwork as "message," let me further explain my use of the word as it applies not only to the camp art, but in my estimation, to all art. I believe that artists use their symbols, whether recognizable or abstract, to put forth their philosophies just as writers use words to express theirs. Henry Moore, one of the great sculptors of our time, said: "Form, the shape of things—is the most exciting side of my life. I do not think in words, I think in shapes."[14] The only limitations artists impose on themselves are the choices made concerning methods of approach, and the use of the "tools of their trade," materially, mechanically, and aesthetically. As soon as artists make a statement— put paint on canvas, mark on paper, chip on stone—they tell us

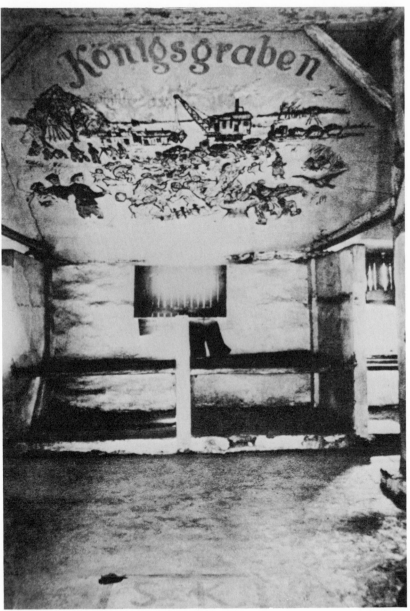

Artist unknown   "Königsgraben," Auschwitz-Birkenau (1945)
Black/white mural (on ceiling of cells), 9′ × 12′
Courtesy Auschwitz Memorial Museum

what they think and feel about the world in which we live. It is a revelation of those things that affect or influence them, and their reactions to the internal or external stimuli. Art is a composite of the intellectual, emotional, and the metaphysical, any one of which can dominate, depending upon the personality and direction of the artist and his or her vision. Art is a matter of understanding and must never be relegated to a matter of taste. The message is ultimately dependent on the knowledge and open-mindedness of the receiver, not on preferences. One need not like a work of art to acknowledge its worth or to understand its meaning. The artists have something to say and give, and in turn they want a response. If this were not so, artists, as well as writers, actors, or musicians, would not exhibit, publish, or perform. It is in a sense an exposition of thought and self—an artistic confessional. The German artist Kathe Kollwitz, an outstanding humanist, was in her seventies when the Nazis came to power. An avid anti-Nazi, she was so harassed and threatened by them that she was forced into seclusion in southern Germany. She wrote: "I am content that my art shall have purpose outside itself. I would like to exert influence in these times when human beings are so perplexed and in need of help."[15]

Humanistic art is also a maverick art. It has existed alongside rather than in the mainstream of the major art movements. It is not a popular art. It is an art that pricks the conscience of the onlooker, intent on expressing humanity and demanding the attention of an audience. Many leading artists at some point in their careers have made strong and searing statements about those elements in their world that they found repugnant or deplorable. The plight of man did not escape the sharp wit and brush of Hieronymus Bosch, or Rembrandt, or Breugel, or Hogarth. Our own times have produced the biting commentaries of the genius Picasso, in his well-known "Guernica" and his lesser-known "Charnel House" (about the Holocaust),[16] and those artists on the international scene who felt compelled to comment on the Holocaust even though they did not experience it: Rico LeBrun's "The Floor of Buchenwald," "Buchenwald Cart," and "Buchenwald Pit"; Gabor Peterdi's "Still Life in Germany"; Jacob Landau's powerful suite of lithographs, "The Holocaust Suite"; Ben Shahn's moving work, "Warsaw, 1943," done in commemoration of the Warsaw Ghetto uprising; Jack Levine's "Rounding Up for the Warsaw Ghetto";[17] and the gripping "Nazi Drawings" of Mauricio Lasansky.

A Place for Artists

The history of the Holocaust is well known. The final solution called for two types of camps: concentration camps and death camps. There were six main extermination centers, all in Poland: Treblinka, Sobibor, Chelmno, Belzec, Maidanek, and the most infamous of them all, Auschwitz, which had forty satellite camps, including Birkenau, Budy and Monowitz, and was often referred to as the "planet Auschwitz." The extermination camps were the ultimate destiny of the Jews and others who were considered *Untermenschen*, via the gas chambers and the ovens. Many other camps had extermination facilities, such as Jasenovac in Yugoslavia; Transnistria in Romania; Mauthausen in Austria; Dachau in Germany; La Risiera di San Sabba in Italy, and "the model camp," Terezin, had a crematorium with four ovens. In the concentration camps the Jews were used for slave labor and exploited for every ability and skill they had until they died from starvation, exhaustion, or became so broken in mind and body that they became *Musselmen* (those whose minds have atrophied, gone dull, along with the deterioration of their bodies). All were eventually to be killed. Hundreds of concentration camps peppered Europe from Norway, Denmark, Holland, Belgium, and Italy, to Greece, from France to the Balkans and the Ukraine. In every country where the Nazi set his boot camps proliferated.

All the Jews were doomed to die, but at different speeds. Considered totally useless, the children, the older people, the maimed and the ill were killed first. The young and healthy, however, were forced to do brute labor. Those with crafts, abilities, or special skills, were exploited as long as they could benefit the Nazi in particular ways. Some of the artists were assigned to the slave labor crews before it was discovered that they had expertise in art. For example, Leo Haas, the Czech artist, was sent to work in the coal mines in Ostrava, Czechoslovakia, until he was recognized by a former official who remembered the portraits he did in the Nisko Collection Center to which they had both been assigned. Halina Olomucki, a young artist, worked in the munitions plant of I. G. Farben in Auschwitz-Birkenau. Alfred Kantor, a young art student, was sent with a crew to help rebuild a bombed munitions plant in Schwarzheide, Germany. The painter Zoran Music worked in the armaments plant that manufactured munitions in Dachau,

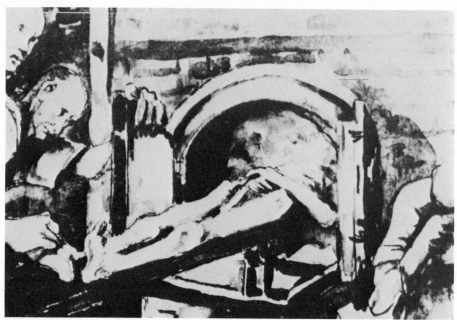

Karol Konieczny   "Im Krematorium," Buchenwald (1945)
Wash drawing
Courtesy Buchenwald Museum

Henri Pieck   "Singende Pferde," Buchenwald (1945)
Charcoal drawing
Courtesy Buchenwald Museum

and Jozef Szajna was sent to work with the construction crews at the Konigsgraben canal at Auschwitz-Birkenau.

Those with specialized skills were exploited until they were no longer useful to the Nazis. Tailors were forced to make Nazi uniforms; locksmiths, goldsmiths, carpenters, shoemakers, and other craftsmen were sought. Dentists, doctors, engineers, architects, and musicians were also compelled to work for the Nazis. Some of the doctors had to assist in the notorious experiments performed on children, women and men. Musicians performed at times in concerts, and often under the most bizarre circumstances. Quartets and ensembles played during a hanging or while prisoners were being marched to the gas chambers. A skilled cellist, Herman Boesson, who was recruited into the Auschwitz orchestra, said: "It saved my life in the camps . . . physically as well as spiritually. The Nazis . . . liked us to play John Phillip Sousa marches during the daily *Appells* [roll calls]. We played STARS AND STRIPES FOREVER while 30,000 inmates marched to work. On Sundays we gave concerts. . . . They gave us instruments which had been stolen."[18]

The Nazis also made a place for the artist. Those who were known artists or who were caught sketching or drawing were either assigned to work in the studio set-up of some of the camps, given particular duties for the pleasure of the Kommandant and his staff, or punished. At times artists were permitted to do their own work, if it was not offensive to the authorities, after the fulfillment of their prison assignments.

In Terezin, for example, provision was made for those who wanted to do artwork but were not assigned permanently to the art studio. The vibrant, active, and eloquent Leo Haas, patriarch of all the surviving artists, was 78 years young when I met him in East Berlin in 1979. Many things impressed me about this man: his capacity for humor (he has been the leading political cartoonist for *Eulenspiegel* publications for years), his positive outlook on life even after six grueling years in such camps as Nisko, Terezin, Auschwitz, Sachsenhausen, and Mauthausen (the low number on his arm proves he was among the first to be sent to the camps), and his willingness to relate to me, with great candor and without bitterness, his harrowing experiences. When I asked him about a little pass I had seen at the Leo Baeck Institute which bore his signature and was issued to Fritz Fabian, an architect from Berlin who had designed theatres, villas, and commercial buildings in Germany and Haifa prior to his arrest and confinement in Terezin, Leo Haas

explained: "For artists or any others to work in the *Zeichenstube*, the art workshop, along with the regularly assigned artists who worked there everyday, a pass had to be issued. It had to be signed by the Kommandant in charge of the artists, and by the chief of the artists, who happened to be me at that time."

In the early stages of the operations in some camps—including those known to be the most wretched and horrible, such as Gurs, Drancy, Compiegne, and Auschwitz—art exhibitions were held. These of course were approved by authorities. In Gurs, located at the foot of the Pyrenees in southern France, particularly noted for abject conditions, exhibitions were held in 1940 and 1941. Isis Kischka not only encouraged artists to do their own work but was responsible for organizing an exhibit in Compiegne, a transit camp outside Paris, near Drancy camp, the largest center for deportation of the Jews from France to the death centers. Kommandant Hoess of Auschwitz decided to have a museum in one of the studios in Auschwitz to show off to the SS elite and visitors to the camp.

In the most unbelievable of places, Auschwitz-Birkenau, contests were held at times for the best decorated barracks. Both Halina Olomucki and Esther Lurie confirmed that women prisoners decorated their barracks and at times were even permitted to have flowers. Dinah Gottliebova-Babbitt painted murals on the walls of the children's temporary barracks in Auschwitz-Birkenau.

The artists were used to do anything in which their expertise was needed, from the making of actual works of art—portraits or landscapes—to graphic and technical works and the most mundane work which could hardly be called "art," such as writing numbers on uniforms.

Range and Background of the Artists

It appears from research that all of the recovered art works were done by professional artists, some on the threshold of very promising careers, teachers of art, commercial artists, cartoonists, students of art, or by those in some field related to art, such as architecture, stage craft, costume design, or crafts. I have come across two exceptions (although there are probably others): Dr. Karel Fleischmann, a doctor, and Peter Loewenstein, a young engineering student. Both were sent to Terezin, both perished in Auschwitz, and both left behind an impressive number of works. The resistance group in Terezin preserved the works of Dr. Fleischmann, and

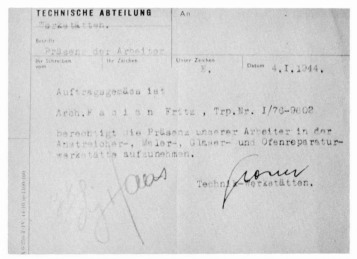

Terezin Pass to Zeichenstube (Art Studio), dated January 4, 1944
Signed by Leo Haas, issued to Fritz Fabian
Courtesy Leo Baeck Institute, New York

Karel Fleischmann   Terezin (1943)
Pen and ink drawing, 18″ × 24″
Courtesy Prague State Jewish Museum

some of the gifts of the period of his confinement during 1942–1944 that survive him are scientific papers, articles on medicine and art history, many poems, and hundreds of drawings of which the Prague State Jewish Museum owns at least two hundred. Among the sixty-one works left behind by Peter Loewenstein, who was eighteen when he was sent with the first contingent of Jews to Terezin, are mainly illustrations he had to do depicting the various industries and products manufactured in Terezin, and graphs and records revealing further statistics about the camps. All are important documents and among them are some of the "secret art" about life in Terezin.

There are many artists who commented on their camp experiences after their liberation. Olly Ritterband, a poet and an artist, now of Denmark, was born in Romania and imprisoned in Auschwitz, Bergen-Belsen and Ravensbruck camps during World War II. She has exhibited internationally in such places as the Nationalmuseet Museum in Copenhagen, Denmark and Ghetto Fighters House, Israel, and was included in the exhibition, "The Jewish Experience in the Art of the Twentieth Century," at the Jewish Museum in New York City. In a letter to me she wrote: "It is of greatest importance to teach and inform today's human beings of what really happened during the Holocaust."[19] Another artist, Elsa Pollack of Israel, imprisoned in Auschwitz, made her powerful and stirring sculptures years after her liberation: "Over the years I kept silent, but I did not forget. . . . The memories urged me on without respite."[20]

Too numerous to list are many Israeli artists, among them the sculptor, Zvi Aldoubi, whose works grace many places in Israel. Although some were not in the ghettos or camps, these artists have made and are still making statements about this horrendous period. Interesting to note is that some of the children-prisoners who miraculously survived have chosen the arts as a profession, among them: Yehuda Bacon and Helga Hoskova who had been in Terezin; Schmuel Bak who had been in the Vilna Ghetto; and Itzak Belfer who was a child in the orphanage of the beloved Janusz Korczak in the Warsaw Ghetto and escaped the trip to the death camp by fleeing to the forests of Poland. Many of the paintings and drawings he produced in later life show the torment and suffering of the Jews in the camps.[21]

The value and importance of this outburst and reaction to the Holocaust by the artists cannot be minimized. Jacob Landau, one of the most eloquent contemporary artists working in America to-day, claims: "The art of confrontation with the real . . . of passion-ate outrage, is both possible and necessary . . . [and] expresses hope and love in the face of terror."[22]

There were creative endeavors throughout the camp system in other areas of the arts of which some were secretive and some were sanctioned by the Nazis for their own purposes. Music programs in the form of symphonies, concerts, and operas for the children as well as adults were given in Terezin, Buchenwald, and Auschwitz (which the SS brazenly attended), and were encouraged in some of the larger ghettos. Drama and other theater productions were held, requiring that stage designs and costumes be made for them. Poets wrote and gave readings, among them the famous poet, Yitzhak Katzenelson, whose poems were hidden and later recov-ered. In the ghettos lectures were given and schools from elemen-tary level to college courses were conducted. Of course, the activi-ties permitted could be stopped immediately upon any whim of the Nazis. Timing for cessation or continuance of any activity was of-ten dependent on "liquidation, resettlement, or selections" of the prisoners.

This flurry of activity in the arts, education, and other areas at-tests to the prisoners' tenacity for life, their indomitable spirit, and their belief in a return to a world of sanity. Theirs was a resistance as strong as the overt rebellions and revolts in the camps of Treblinka, Sobibor, Auschwitz, and the ghettos of Warsaw, Vilna, and the deliberate self-immolation of the smaller ghettos; the se-cret underground and resistance activities; the sabotage of the worker-prisoners; and the heroic efforts of the "littlest resisters"— the children—who ran as couriers and were smugglers of weapons and food. (In the Kovno Ghetto they were garden watchers, and in the Vilna Ghetto they formed children brigades.)

In the beginning, the prisoners were unable to comprehend the enormity or the extent of the destruction and murder awaiting them. As Esther Lurie (one of the artist-suriviors with whom I spoke) said to me:

> When we were sent to the ghetto it seemed at first like a ref-uge after all the indignities and degradations to which we had been subjected during the previous months. We did not envisage what lay ahead. Everything that was happening all around was so strange and peculiar . . . we did not believe it when it did happen [the murders and the killings]. Surely such a thing was impossible.

Frantisek Zelenka Theatre design in Terezin Loft (1942)
Ink drawing
Courtesy Terezin Memorial Museum

How could people anticipate the degree of baseness or the depths to which the Nazi butchery would go? Who would believe this horror: the gas showers, the crematoria, the *Einsatzgruppen* (killing brigades), the experiments, the pits of Ponary and Babi Yar!

The price paid is beyond accounting. We must listen to the voices that cried out, many of them in their last agonies, and heed their warning. The precious spark that the artists generated and the flame of their hope must never be doused. What is unimaginable but real has been recorded for us by these secret artists in a language we can all understand—the language of images. These are the archivists of a visual imagery and pictorial scribes of a macabre world. They portrayed the tragedy as it unfolded before their eyes and as it wracked and absorbed their own bodies and minds. The miracle is here in symbols that will not change with time or aesthetic direction. It is the *yezer hatov* (the good inclination) fighting the *yezer hara* (the evil inclination.) Certainly an ally of these artists would have been Picasso himself, who wrote: "Painting is an instrument of war to be waged against brutality and darkness."[23]

A theatre of horrors, a mob stage,
presenting a caste of unique actors
an unnumerable variety of
characters and faces,
having its own stage-setters and
staff of technicians,
ushers, mess service personnel,
quartermasters, nurses, doctors,
auxiliary services, watchmen,
transport guards and all the people
around, all obeying the waving of a
magic wand.[24]
—*Karel Fleishmann*

Alexander Bogen "Partisans, 1943"
Charcoal drawing, 10″ × 12″
Courtesy A. Bogen

This I tell you, this is a different thing. An immediate reaction without time to think, no time to organize your vision, your style or composition. This was a direct reaction, this art. It is different than being in a studio where you have time to think about style and about expression and about color. This is a different thing. In the circumstances of the Holocaust when you are creative, face to face with the cruel things against you, it is immediate reaction. We had no cameras from this period, only this is left.

Alexander Bogen
Artist-survivor
Tel Aviv, Israel, June 1979

2

The Shackled Artist:
Assigned Art

The artwork produced in the camps and ghettos of Europe between 1939 and 1945 falls into three categories: work assigned by the Nazis and referred to by many scholars and historians as "legal" or official art[1]; clandestine art, the humanistic work that depicted the awful truths of camp existence; and work by a few that was seemingly unrelated to the experiences in the camps.

Assigned Art

The work assigned to artists was done under Nazi supervision and direction. It was partly mechanical and technical. All types of graphic work were needed: maps, charts, graphs, diagrams for construction of roads and buildings, signs, posters, emblems, postcards, and greeting cards. Some of the camp Kommandants had artists do portraits of them, their families, or the staff. Artists were also required to paint landscapes and genre pictures for the Nazis' personal pleasure and for propaganda. In addition, artists were asked to copy masterpieces stolen from the museums of Europe that were intended for eventual resale in Germany and elsewhere. Those artists who were known to be more technically proficient were engaged in making counterfeit money and also in forging such legal documents as passports. Others were forced to render drawings of certain medical "experiments" conducted in some of

Assorted greeting cards, Buchenwald Camp
Courtesy Buchenwald Memorial Museum

Malvina Schalkova "Women's Work Shop — Terezin"
Charcoal drawing, 7½" × 14"
Courtesy Biet Lohamei Haghetoat/Miriam Novitz

the more infamous camps by such people as the notorious Josef Mengele.

The artwork was done in a variety of studios or workshops for groups of artists assigned to these areas or in makeshift arrangements for individual assignments as the need for work arose.

Terezin had a *Zeichenstube* (drawing room) and a *Lautscher Werkstätte* (crafts room). Auschwitz had its "studio" and several craftshops. Sachsenhausen was fully equipped with a drafting room for its counterfeit operations. Mauthausen had crafts workshops and a technical department.[2] Buchenwald had a *Künstlerwerkstätte* (artist workshop). The Bialystok Ghetto, which eventually became a labor camp, had its "Copies Studio." A number of ghettos also had special quarters for artists, such as the Lodz Ghetto where another counterfeit works was in operation, and a graphics department that was staffed by artists. The Kovno Ghetto had a *Mal und Zeichen Werkstätte* (painting and drawing workshop). The Warsaw Ghetto and the Vilna Ghetto were among some of the others where provisions were made to use the artists' abilities in a variety of ways. Actually these compulsory art studios were set up throughout the entire camp network by the Nazis for their own purposes.

Compulsory Studios and Workshops

In Sachsenhausen Concentration Camp[3] near Berlin, and in the Lodz Ghetto in Poland, the SS ran large counterfeit plants. Sachsenhausen was the headquarters of the Gestapo's espionage system and the elite training camp for SS intelligence operations. Artists were forced to reproduce all sorts of legal documents, from British and American currency to passports. The Nazis' plan was to destroy the British and American economies by flooding the market with counterfeit bills. They mainly concentrated on producing copies of the British pound note. Leo Haas, an inmate who had been shifted from place to place, arrived in Sachsenhausen from Auschwitz to do this work. According to him and Reinhard Strecker, a German scholar and historian, the work was done so finely that the money was easily mistaken for the authentic currency. "In fact," said Leo Haas with an amused smile and a mischievous glint in his alert eyes, "a hundred dollar American counterfeit bill which we had just completed was shown to Hitler. He immediately mistook it for the real thing." Eichmann was also fooled. When he fled from the advancing American troops with his prepared stolen loot of gold, jewels, and currency, he said, "I later found out that the foreign currency I got was forged in the course of the big forgery scheme carried out by our counterfeit intelligence."[4]

Counterfeit money and papers also provided an escape route for the fleeing Nazis, with a "lot of help from their friends" such as those who ran the ODESSA (*Organization der SS Angehoerigen* — Association of SS members) and the Monastery Route in Italy, who found their way to the United States and South America.[5]

The counterfeiting scheme was so successful that when Sachsenhausen was evacuated toward the end of the war because of the approaching Russian troops, the "Counterfeit Kommando," as they called themselves, packed up the equipment which the artists had to carry, and fled to Ebensee-Schlier, the satellite of Mauthausen Camp. With the threat of advancing American troops in April 1945, the SS panicked and instead of destroying the equipment and the documents and killing the artists as planned, they fled, taking with them ample amounts of the counterfeit money and necessary documents for their escape. Leo Haas further describes the events of liberation day: "The day that the Allied troops arrived, we were all to have been killed in a forest nearby. The forest had been laid with mines. Fortunately for us, the allied troops arrived earlier than expected, and our lives were saved." Many of those forged documents that were left behind including money, stamps, passports, identification cards, can be seen in the Mauthausen Memorial Museum today, and it is said that some holdings in Switzerland and certain major industries in Germany today used some of this fake money.[6]

Hidden away in the ghetto of Bialystok, a vital textile center in northern Poland, were some of the art works that the Nazis had stolen or confiscated from major museums in the occupied countries and from small collectors and private Jewish citizens. A "Copies Workshop" was organized in Bialystok in which the artist-prisoners were compelled to make reproductions of those works intended for resale in other countries. One of the most ironic and incredible acts of transgression is the fact that Hitler, Goering, and Ribbentrop who were responsible for the banning and destruction of so many great works of art, were now "collecting" art. Selecting for themselves the most prized works and profiting from resale of masterpieces, they perpetrated perhaps the greatest art robbery of all time.[7]

Avid in this pursuit for treasure, Hitler created the *Einsatzstab Rosenberg*, headed by the alleged cultural expert, Alfred Rosenberg; and for Hitler's *Fuhrermuseum* in his birthplace of Linz, Austria, which he hoped to make the art center of the world, he formed his own *Sonderauftrag Linz* (Special Mission Linz) headed initially by Dr. Hans Posse, director of the Dresden Art Gallery. Assisted by a staff of art experts, dealers, and curators, it was the duty of these men to tour the museums and other places in Europe and to confiscate the choicest pieces of work. *Sonderauftrag Linz* amassed for Hitler some 100,000 works of art worth an estimated 300 million dollars, including 10,000 paintings, half of which were old masters. Among them were the *Ghent Altarpiece* by the Van Eycks, Michelangelo's *Madonna and Child*, and works by Vermeer, Breugel, Goya, Rembrandt, and Leonardo Da Vinci.[8] Goering's collection of over 1,300 paintings worth about 180 million dollars contained many of the great works which Goering had labeled as "degenerate art" by such artists as Max Beckman, Marc Chagall, George Grosz, Pablo Picasso, Paul Klee, Vincent VanGogh and Paul Gaugin.[9] While these experts were stormtrooping through the museums of Europe, other SS troops ransacked the homes of Jews in the occupied countries. In this cache of stolen treasure were works confiscated from Jews who could not recover them after the war or who subsequently perished in the ovens of the death camps. The whereabouts of many of the "unclaimed" works are known (such as in the Hofburg in Vienna, Austria), and although many rightful owners have repeatedly asked for their property, delaying tactics have prevailed.[10]

Izak Celniker, an artist-survivor of the "Copies Studio," remembers that among the pieces copied were works by Murillo, Rubens, and Boecklin. About ten artists were employed in this workshop; the head of the group was the Polish artist Abraham Herman. All of the artists were professionals with extensive art experience, and almost all were killed in the "Aktion" in the Ghetto in 1943.[11]

Reproductions were also made in Terezin. Dinah Gottliebova-Babbitt, who was there, wrote:

> I worked in the Olmolerei [art workshop] where postcards of famous paintings were once again transformed into oils. We had two to three days to finish each. To amuse myself, I used to start in one corner and finish in the other. That should give those canvases the value of pictures painted by number.

Eight months after Auschwitz had been set up, Rudolph Hoess, the Kommandant, established an artists' studio for his own use. The artists were expected to produce works of art and handicraft for him, his family, the members of the SS, and their staff. Like his counterparts, Eichmann who was interested in attending the concerts in Terezin, and the "big bosses" who were helping themselves to the art treasures of Europe, Hoess pursued his interest in the culture the prisoners could provide him. He had a small room prepared on the first floor of Block 24 Auschwitz 1, for the "art studio" to be used by the prisoner-artists. At first there were about four or five artists in this studio. As the SS interest in painting, greeting cards, portraits, and landscapes increased, another room was opened in the cellar of Block 4 to accommodate more artists. The SS sent hundreds of prisoners' paintings and postcards out of the camp.[12]

Caught by surprise while sketching one day, Franciszek Targosz—a prisoner who had been riding master in the Polish and Austrian armies—was reported to Hoess. Hoess subsequently appointed Targosz to head the studio in Auschwitz. This was the beginning of the "legal or official" art in Auschwitz.[13]

In the winter of 1941, Hoess decided that KZ Auschwitz 24 should have a museum as well. He decided that a section should display photos and drawings, which could show the inferior racial characteristics of the prisoners. Working on this along with Franciszek Targosz were the artist-prisoners Mieczyslaw Koscielniak and Bronislaw Czech.

Many paintings, drawings, and sculptures from the studios remain, thanks to the efforts of the artists who worked there. According to Henryk Swiebocki, the curator of the Auschwitz Memorial Museum, the collection there includes about five hundred drawings and paintings and sculptures, a rarity for camp art.[14]

In Auschwitz some of the artists were required to draw the victims of Josef Mengele's medical experiments. Coming from Terezin to Auschwitz, Leo Haas was one of those forced, on pain of death, to work for Mengele. He arrived at a time when Mengele was experimenting on twins, trying to make "Aryan types" by changing brown eyes to blue on sets of twins. Thousands of children died as a result of the painful injections he administered without the use of anesthesia.

"I had to draw twins that were very young and some that were very old," commented Leo Haas, in a hushed voice. "I don't know what happened to my drawings but I am sure that all the victims

Artist Unknown   "One Louse — Your Death!," Auschwitz
Warning poster against the much-feared typhus epidemic, posted in barracks
Courtesy Auschwitz Memorial Museum

died. There were five or six of us working at the time." The pain in
Leo Haas' voice was obvious, as he spoke very softly, so we discontinued discussion about the drawings of the experiments.[15]

There were a number of other workshops in Auschwitz. The
carpenters' workshop (*Tischlerei*) produced wooden clogs, spoons,
and later, small wooden carvings. In the metal workshop (*Metallarbeiten*), ink wells, paper weights, letter openers, and other metal
artifacts were made. A locksmith shop produced the German fittings and gear and some souvenirs on order. A camp press room
printed letters and postcards for camp personnel, and order forms,
placards, posters, schedules, and menus for the SS kitchen. A photographic section concentrated on documentary records, but also
manufactured such items as photo albums. In his deposition, Sonderkommando Stanislaw Jankowski describes some of the objects he
built in the furniture workshop: "I was assigned to work making
cupboards, writing tables, and other pieces of furniture." From the
leathercraft shop came many expertly crafted leather goods which
seemed to be the Hoess family's favorite. Many items "in their
pleasant home on the camp grounds surrounded by flower gardens" were done in leather. Even fine leather shoes and gloves were
made for them, some of which were recycled "from the dead prisoners' belongings."[16]

To the Terezin ghetto-camp the cream of the cultural and intellectual world of Czechoslovakia and later other countries were
sent in the early stages of its development. Among them were: Alfred Kantor, art student from Prague; Leo Haas, well-known
graphic artist; Otto Ungar, gentle art teacher from Brno; Bedrich
Fritta, (née Taussig), commercial artist, illustrator, and teacher
from Prague; Felix Bloch; Karel Fleischmann; Petr Kien, artist
and librettist; Adolf Aussenberg; Malvina Schalkova; Charlotte
Buresova; Peter Loewenstein; and Jo Spier, as well as the leading
writers, musicians, and performers of the day.

Terezin was presented to other countries as the "model" camp.
Some of the artists were assigned to work as part of the building
and ground staff. All types of signs, slogans, posters, and placards
had to be made. When the neutral country inspection teams came
to check on how "humanely" the Nazis were treating the prisoners,
the artists had one week to facelift the dismal camp. Leo Haas described how they had to paint the fronts of buildings, the railroad
station, and make street and other signs (such as "Ghetto School,"
"Synagogue," "Restaurant"); fake posters announcing events that

would never take place for billboards that did not exist previously (and would be taken down immediately after the inspection); and dress up shop façades on the outside and make up displays for the inside to make them look used and patronized. All buildings along the route that these inspectors would take were refurbished. As Leo Haas said:

> We artists had no choice, no say; we had to do what we were told or we could be easily "replaced." So we had to set the stage for our common enemy so that they could carry out their charade. We did such an excellent job, that the inspectors did not look further than our excellent stage set. We hoped they would go to the end of the town where the crematorium was hidden away in the fields. We vainly expected they would inquire about the ominous looking quarters at the other end of town, the *Kleine Festung* ["the little fortress," which has its own unique dreadful history] separated from the main camp by a stretch of road and walled in one corner of the garrison town. In fact they were so impressed they went no further than our painted scenario. We did our job, too, too, well; we knew we were very good, and this time we were not very happy about it.

So this group of neutral inspectors bought the "lie of Terezin." Why did they never ask the reason for the imprisonment of Jews in the first place? What was the crime of the children? Leo Haas continued:

> Later, we had to do more technical work, such as making graphs, maps, charts, designs for constructions of roads and buildings and records that were sent monthly to Berlin. The artists needed a place in which to do this work and coordinate the assignments. That is how we were given a room to work in which the Nazis called the *Zeichenstube*. Perhaps because I suggested using another room, or perhaps because I was one of the oldest in the group of artists, I was made the head of the *Zeichenstube*. Sometimes there were as many as twenty artists working at one time. It was by no means a dream of an artist's studio. It was crowded, we had a small light to work by and some tables and chairs. Our supplies were very limited, too. It was not an ideal situation but at least we could work. My main group were my dearest friend, Fritta, Ungar and Bloch. Dr. Fleischmann I knew, but he worked on his own, he never came to the workroom. He was too busy taking care of the many, many sick and he had no medicines.

Peter Loewenstein
"Notions Workshop in Terezin"
(Shows various goods produced in this shop)
Drawing, 9″ × 12″
Courtesy Gerda Korngold

Peter Loewenstein
"Chart of Notions Workshop," Terezin Camp
(Shows production of materials with
actual sample swatches) 9″ × 12″
Courtesy Gerda Korngold

Leo Haas   "Zeichenstube in Terezin" (art studio)
Pen and ink drawing, 7″ × 10″
Courtesy Terezin Memorial Museum

Peter Loewenstein
Development and expansion of the
Terezin Ghetto   Chart, 8″ × 10″
Courtesy Gerda Korngold

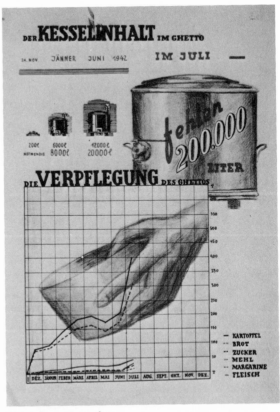

Peter Loewenstein
Food supply, capacity, and consumption in the
Terezin Ghetto (1941)   Chart, 9″ × 12″
Courtesy Gerda Korngold

In the summer it was very hot especially when we were crowded, and in the winter we had no heat. As time went on the artists had to do other work such as paint pictures for the kommandants and the other SS who demanded them. We tried to assign work to the artists who had expertise in particular areas for as time went on the SS wanted portraits of themselves, landscapes and still lifes. They also wanted scenes of Terezin town to show what a "model" camp was [such as the work of Fritz Fabian]. It was all propaganda.

We all realized soon enough what was happening on the outside. With the transports of prisoners passing in and out of our camp, a grapevine of information developed which the prisoners carried with them always by word of mouth [since] we knew too well the risks of being caught with written messages. All kinds of news passed on in this way: about the war, family, the death camps, and this is how, after my friends and I were tortured and beaten after our secret work was discovered, some of my friends in Auschwitz were expecting me. They knew I was coming and on which transport I would be arriving. They were actually waiting for Leo Haas.

While in Terezin we knew that we could prolong our lives if we kept working. We also knew that the Nazis at any moment could decide it was our turn to go, so we had ideas about getting messages out to the world in the event none of us survived. We were so oppressed by the horrible surrounding that we devoted ourselves to our office duties in the day, and then night after night, gathered in our darkened workroom, we drew our works telling what the Nazis were really doing and they matured as a cycle. This is how Fritta did his great cycle of 150 drawings and how Ungar, Bloch and I did ours. Then we hid them and when I went back after liberation, I found all the works intact. We would take turns standing watch in case Keidl, the SS official in charge of us, would check on us. We always dreaded his visits to our workroom. However, it was not the SS Keidl who found out about us, it happened another way.

Under the dubious protection of night and the tension created by fear of discovery by their dreaded boss, Keidl, these four good friends have left a most gripping and heartrending body of works revealing the deception and the horror of Terezin.

There was another workshop in Terezin called the *Lautscher Werkstätte,* referred to by some of the prisoner-artists as the *Lautschana.* This was in operation from March 1942 to September 1943, and the SS ordered the Czech, Oskar Perschke, to be its head. From this workshop came a variety of artifacts: dolls, lamps, toys, leather goods, artificial flowers, and many other kinds of hand-crafts which the Nazis sold outside the camp. The excellent draw-ings of Peter Loewenstein showing the various items and the types of products made here reveal the extent of this workshop's opera-tions. The drawings are so graphic, they were probably used for ad-vertisements for purchasers of the available objects.

The painter Charlotte Buresova also worked in this workshop for a time. The sculptor, Arnold Zadikow, whose life work was al-most entirely destroyed by the Nazis as decadent Jewish art, was as-signed here, as was his wife, a painter of miniature watercolors, Helena Zadikow, for the short time the shop was in operation. When the *Lautscher Werkstätte* was liquidated, Oskar Perschke was deported to Flossenburg, where he perished.[17]

The Nazis set up a *Mal und Zeichen Werkstätte* — a graphics and art workshop — in the Kovno Ghetto. The function of this shop was to make signs, placards, announcements, and directives for the *Arbeitseinsatz*, for the Jews who were confined to the Ghetto, and to fill assignments that required drawing or artwork of any kind.

Individual Assignments

Many artists were given work on an individual basis that covered a wide gamut of activities from specific projects ordered by the camp officials to work for the pleasure and use of Nazi personnel. Since the artists in these cases did work as the occasion demanded, most often they did not have studios in which to work. Such was the case for Simon Wiesenthal, head of the famed Documentation Center in Vienna. From Janowska concentration camp in 1941, Wiesen-thal and his wife were sent to the special forced-labor camp that served the Ostbahn Repair Works (Eastern Railroad). He was or-dered to replace the Soviet symbols and paint swastika and eagle shields on the captured Russian locomotives. After a time he was promoted to sign painting. When it was discovered that he was an architect, Wiesenthal was assigned to work as a technician and draftsman. So highly regarded and respected was his work that Oberinspektor Kohlrautz of the camp permitted him to go into the nearby town to purchase and select his own supplies for his techni-cal work. At times Kohlrautz would affix his own signature to Si-mon Wiesenthal's drawings before turning them over to the offi-cials.

In preparation for the celebration of Hitler's fifty-fourth birth-day on April 20, 1943, Wiesenthal was told to paint posters and

Artist unknown   Spice jar, Terezin
Wood, 4″ high
Courtesy Leo Baeck Institute, New York

Artist unknown   Stuffed toy, Terezin
(Made in craft workshop)
Courtesy Terezin Memorial Museum

Simon Wiesenthal Mauthausen Camp (1945)
Drawing
Courtesy Simon Wiesenthal

Artist unknown   Poster, "Wash hands before eating"
Rough copy in charcoal and pastel, 9″ × 12″
Courtesy Leo Baeck Institute, New York

swastikas for the camp SS. One day he was ordered to stop because his name was included in the roundup of Jews to be executed that day. He had already gone with the others down *der Schlauch* (the hose), from which it was reputed no one ever returned, and was standing naked on the edge of the sand pit, the shots of the executioners ringing in his ears, when he heard his name being called. He was ordered to put on his clothes (which he had to find in a pile he was not to disturb), taken back to headquarters, and told that they needed more signs completed by that afternoon for the celebration. A big poster was also needed, in accord with these specific instructions: "Paint a swastika on a red background and in white letters the words, *WIR DANKEN UNSEREM FUHRER* (We thank our Fuhrer)."[18]

The Israeli painter, Halina Olomucki, an attractive and petite woman today, also painted signs for the Nazis. She was a teen-ager when she was sent along with her family to the ghetto in the city of her birth, Warsaw. After great suffering in the ghetto, three days of waiting without food or water in the *Umschlagplatz* (collection center for deportation), she was sent on a "transport herded like cattle with no room to sit or stand" to Maidanek Death Camp just south of Warsaw. From there she was sent to Auschwitz-Birkenau. When that camp was liquidated on January 18, 1945, she was one of those who marched on foot for two days without any sustenance to Ravensbruck[19] in Eastern Germany.

Halina Olomucki was sent to Block 10. When the SS were looking for an artist to paint slogans and signs for the barracks and it was discovered that Halina could draw, she was assigned this task. The signs and slogans were either directives or were used for decoration. Many of them were cruelly deceptive and a mockery to the prisoners. For example: "Wash your hands before eating" (there was not enough water to drink let alone any for washing), and "To the Latrines" (which were hardly latrines at all, and never worked). Halina explained that "The SS would give me materials with which to work, and once I was even given aquarellas [watercolors]. Occasionally they would bring me an extra ration of bread. Even the guards would slip me a piece of bread for a sketch. But while I was doing this, I would use the material to make sketches about what was happening to us."

Despondent over the loss of her entire family, distressed by the unbearable conditions, aching from the beatings and weak from starvation, Halina had to work in the women's slave labor unit as well. She was assigned to work in the munitions plant, and here she was also active in "other things." When plans for a revolt were made known to her and her help was requested, she agreed and was one of the women who smuggled out munitions powder, hidden in her clothing, a little at a time. Although risky and dangerous, Halina says she *had* to aid her comrades. The rest is history. Halina was involved in the revolt in October 1944 which resulted in the destruction of Crematorium 111, in which several SS guards were killed and some of the revolutionaries caught. Throughout the brutal corporal tortures, not one of these revolutionaries revealed the identities of the others. The surviving prisoners were forced to stand at exhaustive roll call in the *Appellplatz* and watch their friends' murders—and had to stand there long after their friends had expired.

Block 1 to Block 10 in Auschwitz-Birkenau housed the women who were in the work crews. When Dr. Clauberg was appointed head of Block 10, it was turned into an experimental station for medical atrocities.[20]

Halina's response about the dates of her stay in Birkenau was stinging and numbing: "Block 10, madame, Block 10, do you realize what was Block 10!"[21] Only a gentle remonstrance from the soft voice of her husband, Bolek, himself a survivor, eased the frenzy and agitation in her voice, and she continued more calmly:

I was beaten on my head so many times; it was pummeled and pummeled, so I can't remember dates or the names of streets, or things like that. But I can still see everything, I can still smell all the horrible odors, and I could take you to the exact places. After the war I went back to my bunk and found my work. I can draw from memory all the people, the suffering young girls. When I think about it, I am there not here, I still feel the terror, the fear, but the dates, those things I do not remember.

Although Dinah Gottliebova-Babbitt worked in the art shop in Terezin, she also had to do individual assignments. As she said, "I spent a lot of time at the stables painting horses, some for the foreman, Karl Klinger and for his friend, Karel Pollak. The SS then ordered copies, which I produced with apelike speed. This earned me status and more lucrative jobs like fruit picking and herding sheep."

She describes an unusual assignment requested in Auschwitz-Birkenau by the block leader of a large group that had come from Terezin together:

My career as survivor began in Auschwitz-Birkenau by decorating the children's barracks to their specifications with Disney's Snow White and the Seven Dwarfs in giant size on the inner walls.[22] The murals were done at the request of Freddie Hirsh who was my friend and the head of the Children's Day Block, and the Terezin unit. He also furnished the paint. Many visiting old timers and SS men demanded of Fred to have various things drawn and painted.[23]

A number of individual artists also had to do portraits. While in Nisko Collection Center, Leo Haas did pencil portraits of the officials. Halina Olomucki recalled that in Auschwitz, "From time to time the SS and even the guards would come to me to do something for them from photos, or they would ask me to do some small sketches, and often their portraits." Ella Lieberman Shiber arrived in Auschwitz from the Bedzin Ghetto as a teen-ager. While she was standing in line, an SS officer asked if there were an artist in the group. Ella was singled out as one by a prisoner, and was given a photograph to copy, of an official's son who had been killed. Her work proved satisfactory and she was assigned to make portraits.

Dinah Gottliebova had described her last assignment in Neustadt-Gleue, which was the last stop after the death march that began on January 21, 1945:

> There, shortly before the liberation, about a month before or so, the SS cook (a young woman) wanted a picture of her missing in action husband painted from a photograph. I was called into the kitchen and put to work there with my mother and friend, Alexandra, peeling potatoes and turnips. This incredible windfall came at a time when we were no longer fed daily, but every other day or so and my mother could no longer stand up at roll call, so Alexa and I had to hold her up between us. But the crappy portrait saved all three of us.

Another artist who painted portraits in the concentration camp was Arnold Daghani, born in Bucovia, Romania, which was annexed to the Soviet Union in 1941 but later recaptured by the Romanians and the Germans. The Jews were brutally massacred there and many were sent to the camp called Transnistria in the Ukraine. This was an enormous complex, situated between the Bug and the Kniester Rivers, north of Odessa. In her history of the Holocaust, Nora Levin describes these camps as among the most appalling in Europe. . . . Some inmates were seen running around naked, eating grass and potato peelings. . . . the Jews in that camp were fed on a diet of cattle food that resulted in paralysis.

Leo Haas   Schrader Portrait,   Nisko (1939)
Pencil drawing, 6″ × 8″
Courtesy Leo Haas

Bogdanovka of this concentration camp compound was the greatest death center in Romania."[24] Given paints and paper, Daghani painted portraits of the Nazis and the guards. He is the only known painter to have worked on his art here. His secret work was done in a room where a sympathetic guard permitted him to work.[25]

Dinah Gottliebova also worked in the Medical unit of Auschwitz. She was ordered by the *Lagerarzt* Mengele to do portraits of gypsies, *Zigeuner-Portraits*. He wanted them for his *Pseudowissenschaftlichen Rasseforschungen* (false medical experiments of racial types). These portraits were done in watercolors provided by Mengele. After the portraits were completed, most of the gypsies were gassed and incinerated in the crematoria. Some of the portraits were photographs, some drawings, and some paintings. Of the twelve portraits completed by Dinah Gottliebova, seven have been salvaged. Among them were portraits of gypsies from Germany, France, Poland, and two of young women, and one of a young boy. These are rare and vitally important for documenting the tragedy that befell the gypsies of Europe. They, like the Jews, were considered *Untermenschen* and served as Mengele's guinea pigs.

The entire transport on which Dinah had arrived from Terezin was sent to the gas chambers on March 8, 1944. She and her mother were spared, along with a "few sets of twins, one doctor, two nurses, and four more people who were useful in his [Mengele's] studies because he still needed us."

In many cases artists were assigned to do work that was only remotely related to anything that could be construed as "art." For example, Esther Lurie was assigned to the *Innendienst* (internal service of the camp) in Leibitz. She was the *Nummerschreiberin*, which simply meant that she had to rewrite the faded numbers on the sleeves of the prisoners' uniforms. In Dachau, some of the artists wrote the prisoners' numbers with *Tintenstift* (ink) on the corpses as they were crammed into common coffins.

Art for Barter

Occasionally guards and other camp personnel would befriend or bribe the artists to do work for them in exchange for a morsel of bread or for pencils or paper. A well-developed barter system existed in some of the camps. Leo Haas has explained that some prisoners in Terezin were assigned to such tasks as working in the kitchens serving the SS guards. Having access there to such things as bread, jam, and sometimes a piece of horsemeat, the artists could "trade" their works for these precious items with the kitchen workers. One of the housekeepers for the chief SS barracks in Tere-zin exchanged jam, cigarettes, and other "scarce" items for the works of the artist-prisoners. During her time in Terezin she col-lected and still owns some of the finest artwork done there. In Gu-sen, Aldo Carpi exchanged his sketch with an SS official for ciga-rettes.

This barter system could not have passed unnoticed by the Nazi watchdog sentinels. A double-edged activity for profit and for pun-ishment, the guards as well as the SS benefited by this exchange of art and goods and money: "Those who undertook to forward illegal letters were also liable to suffer reprisal, including imprisonment in a camp. It happened occasionally that an SS man would agree to transmit illegal correspondence, not out of pity, but for remunera-tion in cash, food, or other things."[26]

Often, artists who were caught off-guard sketching would be punished. Esther Lurie, in the Kovno Ghetto in Latvia in 1941, sent from there to Stutthof-Nauen Camp in 1944, and then to Leibitz, a women's slave labor camp in eastern Germany, recounts that while she was sketching in Leibitz, a guard spotted her. Hav-ing experienced beatings for sketching, she was frightened and put away her work. She recalls:

> I was beaten many times for drawing when I got caught. In the camps I had scarcely any opportunity of sketching. Dis-cipline was exceedingly strict, and we were always under ob-servation. Anyway, the guard approached me, I was ready for a beating. Instead he asked to see what I was doing, and asked me to do a portrait of him for his family. When I fin-ished he was so pleased that he came to see me later and brought me paper and pens. Up to that time I did my draw-ings with ink and chips of wood. As a result of this incident in Leibitz other Nazis came to me for the same reason. One of them brought to me a photograph of his child and wanted me to copy it. It turned out very well and he was so pleased that he brought me an extra ration of soup.

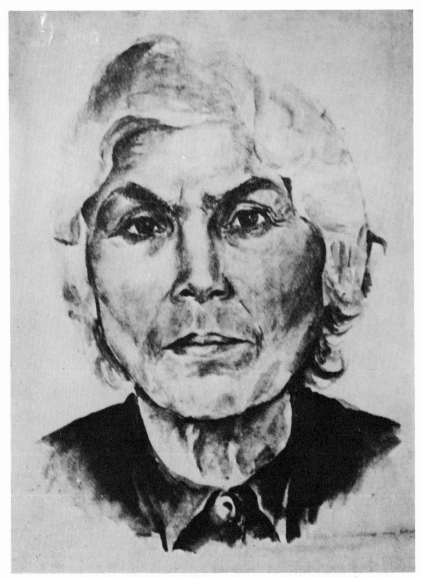

Dinah Gottliebova (Babbitt)   "German Gypsy," Auschwitz Camp (1944)
Watercolor, 8" × 10"
Courtesy Auschwitz Memorial Museum

Dinah Gottliebova (Babbitt)
"Portrait of a Dutch Gypsy," Auschwitz-Birkenau (1944)
Watercolor, 8″ × 10″
Courtesy Auschwitz Memorial Museum

Dinah Gottliebova (Babbitt)
"Polish Gypsy," Auschwitz Camp (1944)
Watercolor, 7″ × 9″
Courtesy Auschwitz Memorial Museum

Dinah Gottliebova (Babbitt)
"Portrait of a Gypsy," Auschwitz Camp (1944)
Watercolor, 8″ × 6″
Courtesy Auschwitz Memorial Museum

Other artists who survived recall experiences similar to Esther Lurie's. Alfred Kantor, an art student of eighteen, was sent in 1941 to Terezin to prepare it as a camp. Imprisoned there until 1943 when he was sent on a transport to Auschwitz, where, he recounted,

> it was difficult to get paper and pencil but I managed. A physician permitted me to hide in the hospital barracks so that I could sketch and draw. Jewish doctors were assigned to work in the infirmaries by the SS. One of the doctors gave me a tiny watercolor set to use. He also gave me some paper, and I remember painting small pictures of Prague street scenes for him.

Toward the end of the war, in February of 1945, the reknowned Nazi-hunter, Simon Wiesenthal, by profession an architect, arrived in Mauthausen concentration camp, near Hitler's hometown in Austria, with a convoy of other prisoners from Buchenwald. One of the most dreaded of camps, Mauthausen was reputed to have a maximum survival time for prisoners of three days.[27]

Weighing barely one hundred pounds, and not expected to live, Simon Wiesenthal was assigned to Block VI, the death block. He describes how the guard there found out that he was an architect and asked him to do designs for a coffeehouse he planned to open after the war; "I made detailed drawings for the coffeehouse. I even designed costumes for the waiters. Lying on my bunk, I drew so many plans that they made up quite a book. The guard was very happy and brought me more bread."[28]

Simon Wiesenthal   Mauthausen Camp (1945)
Drawing, Mixed media
Courtesy Simon Wiesenthal

Art for Resistance groups

Besides exchanging works for food and other materials, there were other purposes the artists used for their work. Those who were doing technical drawings or working on secret documents whose revelation would mean vulnerability to attacks and attempted espionage by the underground, would pass these plans on whenever possible to the resistance groups. Sometimes these plans also aided in saving lives.

In September 1942, Simon Wiesenthal was still technician at the Ostbahn Repair Works, and he and his wife were by this time the only surviving members of his family. He was determined to save her life, believing that he too would soon go to his death. He had just witnessed the deportation of his sixty-three-year-old mother, who was herded into the cattle cars with other old women. He could only stand helplessly by while the cars remained in the burning August sun, at the railyards where he worked, for three days with no one permitted to give food or water to the old women. He could hear them begging for water. (The cars eventually went to Belzec death camp in Poland where all the women perished.) For this reason he approached his friends in the Polish underground who he knew were planning to blow up the Lwow railroad junction, and offered to draw maps showing all the potentially vulnerable points. Because Wiesenthal had set up his office in a small wooden hut on the site of the railroad works where he fulfilled his technical assignments, he was able secretly to draw maps of the junction. In exchange he asked the underground to take his wife out to safety. The deal was arranged and his wife survived.[29]

Jerzy Adam Brandhuber made detailed and precise drawings for the resistance group in Auschwitz. Born in Cracow, Poland, he was a well-known Polish artist and professor of art. When the Nazis overran Poland in 1939, he joined the underground and was captured. Sent to Auschwitz, he worked with the artists. He was approached by his colleague Benek Swierczyna of the resistance movement and asked to do detailed drawings of Birkenau, the entire camp complex, including the crematorium, the *Appellplatz* (roll call center), for the revolt that was being planned. He wrote: "I made diagrammatic and written outlines for the resistance."[30] Jozef Szajna furnished the Polish underground with secret technical drawings that he did in the factory where he was forced to work. The work done by the artists of the camps was dependent on the

Kommandants' decisions about what was essential and what would be profitable. "The real ruler of every concentration camp is the officer in charge of the prison camp. The commandant may leave his stamp upon the outer form of communal life, and this will be more or less obvious according to the energy and enthusiasm he devotes to his job. It is he who directs policy, has formal authority, and bears ultimate responsibility for all that happens."[31] Whenever an artist's hand was needed, it was exploited, and then like all the others who perished in the ovens of the death camps, so did many of the artists when they outlived their usefulness. There were no choices for the artists—it was do or die. If the artists tried to conceal their professions it could mean death for not revealing all the facts about themselves.

Squandered Gifts

Specialized skills or professional work were not always safeguards for prolonging life. In some cases, it hardly mattered. Not all the artists were assigned studio work, and many died, like thousands of other inmates, from the barbaric working conditions, or were like countless others, murdered.

Budy, a satellite of Auschwitz situated about four kilometers away from it, was a farm prison where 300 to 400 women were incarcerated. They were the slave-labor farm units and worked the once-abandoned farms. Many were French Jewesses, some Ukrainians, and some Polish who were very well educated and not rebellious so that there was no reason to electrify the single wire fence that surrounded their hovels in Budy, nor was the camp brightly illuminated at night, as were so many other camps, to discourage attempts at escape. Yet it was here that one of the bloodiest massacres occurred. Most of the French women belonged to intellectual circles, some had studied at the Sorbonne, and some were artists. Most were killed one autumn night when hysterical women guards, with the help of a few male guards, turned on the women prisoners in a frenzy. No explanation has ever been found for this butchery.

Kommandant Hoess, not incapable of the worst brutality himself, comments: "The Budy bloodbath is still before my eyes, I find it incredible that human beings could ever turn into such beasts. The way . . . the French Jewesses were knocked about, tearing them into pieces, killing them with axes and poles. The heads of some of them had been completely severed and some had died after being thrown out of the windows."[32]

Aat Breur
"Death of a Friend," Ravensbruck Camp (1945)
Charcoal drawing, @ 7" × 9½"
Courtesy Ravensbruck Memorial Museum

Jadwiga Simon-Pietkiewiczowa
Ravensbruck Camp (1943)
Charcoal Drawing, 4½" × 3"
Courtesy Janina Jaworska

Hoess, however, did not hesitate to have a group of artists shot and hanged. Held as hostages in Auschwitz, where they had been sent after being accused of attempting to kill a high-ranking SS officer at the airport in Rakowice near Cracow,[33] 198 artists were arrested in a Cracow artist's café on April 24–25, 1942, and brought to Auschwitz.

In May 1942, the SS shot eleven artists in Auschwitz for not completing several works in time for Himmler's visit to the camp. From all reports, no one informed the artists involved that there was a deadline.[34]

Those artists who did assigned work were at times able to prolong their lives, which in some cases meant salvation. Dinah Gottliebova-Babbitt explains with great candor: "It never occurred to me to smuggle anything out of Auschwitz. I didn't think anybody cared what happened to us. I just used my ability to draw to save my life."

Osias Hofstatter   Camp de Gurs (1941)
Charcoal drawing, 6″ × 10″
Courtesy Osias Hofstatter

I *can't understand it, what had happened. I can understand the Christians who have not passed by these things, who don't believe that it happened, truly. I can't not believe it because I passed through it. I lost my parents—I lost almost everything. But to understand it, why man in all history especially in our time has making so much cruelties; I can't understand why it happened but that it happened—that people are even denying it in Germany, the neo-Nazis, this is a crime to heaven. And although I would like to put the Holocaust behind me, lately, I am thinking of mother and father who perished, and sufferance has been the center, the core, of my art.*

Osias Hofstatter
Artist-survivor
Ramat Gan, Israel, June 1979

3

The Secret Artists: Clandestine Art

The most remarkable of all the artwork done in the camps was done secretly and then hidden—the clandestine art. The determined efforts of the artists to take advantage of any opportunity, even at great risks to themselves, is in itself an incredible tale beyond accounting. As ineffable as the Holocaust is to describe, so is this phenomenal activity by a group of artists while imprisoned in the camps. It is also remarkable that so much of this work has been salvaged and can now be seen in museums, archives, and private collections throughout the world. It is sought by curators and private collectors as well. Vital as historical documentation, some of this work attained artistic excellence as examples of humanistic art.

Conditions in the Camps

In the camps, the most unlikely atmosphere for anything productive, and especially anything creative, thousands of pieces of art were produced and have been recovered. The artists secretly struggle to expose the extremity and depth of inhuman conditions.

Although we cannot adequately determine how mental anguish was expressed through the art, the conditions of deprivation were clearly reflected in the clandestine art done by the prisoners. Well documented are the efforts by the Nazis to dehumanize their prisoners before putting them to death. Hunger, disease, torture, and

53

Bedrich Fritta   Terezin Camp (1943)
Pen and ink drawing, 18″ × 24″
Courtesy Thomas Fritta Haas

Leo Haas
"Hanging," Auschwitz Camp
Charcoal drawing, 16″ × 20″
Courtesy Terezin Memorial Museum

killings were the daily companions of these ravaged people. The physical privations—starvation, congestion, lack of water and toilet facilities, lack of clothing (or misfitted clothing adding to the bizarre appearance of the wasted prisoners), exhaustive labor, and beatings—were compounded by psychological torments.

Prisoners were kept in a state of frenzy, uncertainty, tension, and fear. They were forced to observe hangings, shootings, selections, wrenching separations, and to obey humiliating and often contradictory orders. Babies were actually ripped from mothers' arms and flung to the ground, into the flames, or into the pits. A common practice was to change rules without notice to destroy the emotional equilibrium of the victims and exact reprisals and punishment of the most unreasonable and insane kind. There were senseless calisthenics that had no meaning but to gratify the sadism of the tormentors.

Accounts of camp conditions can be found in many books on the Holocaust, but the descriptions by the artists are among the most expressive to be found anywhere. Esther Lurie describes most eloquently two of the many incidents that occurred to her in the camps:

> Our greatest hardship was winter. We wrapped every rag round our bodies cutting off strips for hand, foot, and head-gear. We were worst off for the foot wear. We twisted straw into clogs or made something out of scraps sewn together. Frostbite was a common ailment with little or nothing at all round one's feet. In none of my drawings do real shoes appear. Soup bowls were very precious. If we didn't have them we didn't get our soup. So we tied them to our bodies so that they wouldn't be stolen from us and to keep our hands free to wield the shovel which was very heavy for a woman. This shovel we had to carry to a work site which could be three to four miles from our camp. In my drawings the soup bowls appear tied to the women. This is truly how it was.

She continued about another incident:

> We were issued one pair of socks between two people. When we worked in the winter we had to take off our coats because they would hamper our movements and interfere with our work. One day a woman did not take hers off, and before she could explain she was kicked and beaten. After the beating her coat was removed. There was nothing underneath. This was in the cold of winter. This time even the *Oberscharführer* was surprised. I longed to record on paper all that I saw. Yet the presence of the camp commandant,

Oberscharführer Olk, nicknamed the *Schnabel* (Beak), filled the soul with dread and fear. I could not spend much time at it [drawing].

Most poignantly, Zoran Music wrote about conditions in Dachau, where he was imprisoned:

During the day we could not remain indoors. We were in filth, exposed to the cold, the cadavers piled everywhere. At noon soup. The skeleton still standing and grasping his bowl between his hands searches for a place to eat it. He finds a free spot on the head of a corpse—drinks the liquid which is not thick but at least warm. He does not realize where he sat nor where he placed his crumb of bread made of sawdust and potatoes.

Music continued about his experiences:

The arrival of a transport in open cattle cars. The dead fall out. The voyage lasted a long time, without food, without drink, hermetically sealed, some gone mad were screaming, eyes protruding out of their heads. Enveloping all was an indescribable odor of decomposition and filth.

Halina Olomucki relates an incident she witnessed in the Ravensbruck Camp for women:

It was very cold, and the women had to carry the soup to the barracks in vats. One day the soup spilled to the ground in front of our barracks. When they slipped, the soup spilled and froze to the ground. As bad as it was we knew this meant no food for us that day, so the women threw themselves upon the frozen mess and licked it up like dogs.

Of Gurs Camp, Osias Hofstatter recalled:

It was such a filthy place. The first night I came to Gurs from St. Cyprien, I couldn't sleep, and St. Cyprien was bad enough. It all looked so hopeless. I fell to the floor shaken with fever. It was such a horrible place infested with rats and lice. There were no beds for us. We had to sleep on the earthen floor which became muddy when it rained. Often we were afraid to sleep at all because the rats were known to nibble on anything that protruded and many noses got nibbled on. Finally we got so exhausted we would fall into a restless sleep. When it rained the clay soil would get as slick as ice. The older people could not manage to walk on it, and many would slip and fall to the ground. No one was allowed to help them. Many remained there until they died or were able to crawl back to their miserable sheds.

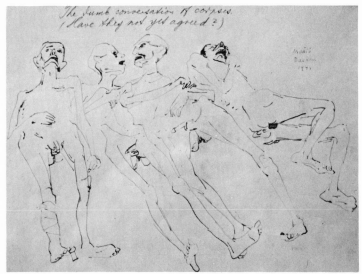

Zoran Music   Dachau Camp (1944)
Pen and ink drawing, 10″ × 12″
Courtesy Dr. Marcus Smith

Osias Hofstatter   "Gurs Barracks," Camp de Gurs (1941)
Pen and ink drawing, 5″ × 7″
Courtesy Osias Hofstatter

Agnes Lukacs Auschwitz-Birkenau
Pen and ink drawing
Courtesy Sachsenhausen Memorial Museum

Pierre Mania "A la Corridre," Buchenwald Camp (1944)
Drawing
Courtesy Sachsenhausen Memorial Museum

Alfred Kantor was in the labor group paving roads: "We were ordered to carry heavy rocks and stones for miles to pave the road one truck could have done in a fraction of the time. Most of us already half starved became deathly ill. My mother was on the woman's detail, of the same project, and one day I passed her and she was carrying rocks like all the rest of us." She perished soon after in the gas chambers.

Alexander Bogen saw, "forsaken children. We saw people being taken for slaughter. I could not let my pencil fall, an artist doomed to death recording and so preserving those doomed to death."[1]

At the outbreak of the war in 1939, Jozef Szajna joined the Polish underground and was caught while trying to escape and sent to Auschwitz in 1941. He was assigned to work with the penal crew on the construction of the canal to drain the ever-present marsh waters from Birkenau to the Vistula. He wrote: "Konigsgraben [the canal] was a sweat shop. We trampled side by side in mire so deep that we got cramps in our legs. It was so cold and damp tramping in the mud, I thought I could stand it no longer or that I would not come through it. It was unbearable. After three weeks, I got typhus and was sent to the camp hospital."[2]

Despite these conditions, the artists continued working. It became their mission, a burning need that impelled them to work under duress, pain, anguish, and the spectre of death. These works cry out of the depths of that warped hell on earth like warnings: "unless the artist is listened to we are likely to forget that not the beast but the human is both cause and object of the inhuman."[3]

The Dangers

By their own accounts, the risks taken by the artists were extreme, as were the conditions under which they dared to work. To be caught meant certain death, not only to those involved but also to other prisoners who may not have known anything of the activity. Nazi reprisals are common knowledge. As Avraham Golub-Tory has explained: "The task was dangerous, for the Nazis refused to permit any documentation of their depravity. A man could be hung for possessing the wrong photograph. A Jew could be shot for a poem."[4] Leo Haas has reflected, "Perhaps it is only today that I realize the great danger we were working under. We had to use greatest caution in drawing and hiding them [the drawings] from the SS."

Esther Lurie recounts her experience in Leibitz: "I had to be careful not to be seen or caught sketching by the Nazi guard. The hope of remaining alive was so faint, still less could I hope that the drawings would be left in my possession, even if I were to succeed in evading death. . . . These few drawings I hid in my clothes for the time I spent in Leibitz."[5] Alfred Kantor also wondered, in reflection, at his daring: "On looking back, I realized that taking it upon myself to expose Auschwitz with my drawings could only have come while still very young and capable of being so brazen despite the bleakest of circumstances."[6]

In the neat home of Anna and Osias Hofstatter in Israel, surrounded by orderly racks of art works and bookshelves full of the beloved authors Osias quoted with ease—Goethe, Mann, Freud, and Wiesel (whose work he admired very much, calling *Night* a flawless work)—I had the privilege of enjoying their hospitality and speaking with the gentle philosopher-artist. We talked at length about his philosophy, art, critics, and camp experiences. With the gift of simplicity and candor that comes only from one who has suffered much and has thought much, Osias explained: "I made quick sketches and to this day I sketch quickly even though I don't have to. Since my time in the camp I can work no other way now."

Alexander Bogen, who fought with the partisan units in the Narocz Forest and slipped in and out of the Vilna Ghetto to recruit young people to join the partisans, told me: "I recorded in telegram style, so to say, while on my way to some action, leaning over my rifle or standing tensely in ambush. Often as I waited in my secret hideout in Vilna I would draw the scene below me in the street."

Aldo Carpi of Milano, Italy, was sent to Gusen, Mauthausen, in 1944. He had done a group of paintings entitled, Arriva L'Uragano ("The Hurricane Comes"), which depicted the horrors of war. While in Gusen he kept a diary, *Il Diario di Gusen*, which he illustrated with sketches of the atrocities of that camp. He wrote:

When I started to write these letters, my roommates asked me what I was writing. . . . A young man said, " You write? Don't you know it is absolutely forbidden to write or to possess any writings in your pocket? You are playing with your life. If they find these notes your are lost. The minimum sentence is twenty-five whip or club lashes on your back. . . . Otherwise you pay with your life. . . . Works such as yours are considered even more dangerous."[7]

Why all this fear and secrecy? Why the frenzy of the Nazis to destroy any evidence of their genocide? In their minds, when the thousand-year Reich became a reality there was not to be a trace, or a clue as to how it became *Judenrein*. In their corrupt scheme, they hoped to eliminate all evidence of the obliteration of the Jewish people. Drawings and records of their crimes by the artists were dangerous and could be lethal to their plan.

The Motive

The artists of the camps were driven by a desire to convey scenes of the truth—the everyday life of the camps—a life so grotesque that to many it is still incredible, but the evidence is here in these drawings.

From interviews and other documentation of the surviving artists, there is no doubt about their purpose and their mission. Halina Olomucki recalls:

> My intention was to leave documents about the destruction of my people. . . . My fellow prisoners wanted me to draw but for a different reason: "If you live to leave this hell make your drawings tell the world about us, we want to be among the living at least on paper. All this suffering and death must be known." And this need to document became an extraordinary force that carried me to survival, just as painting saved my life.

For Alfred Kantor, "Sketching took on a new urgency. I was determined to keep a continuous record even though I knew there was no chance to take these out. I started to sketch continually almost anything that came to my eye. It was not so much that I wanted to draw my own story, but rather to capture this extraordinary place so that I could show the world something of it, when and if, I was ever free." Osias Hofstatter told me that while in Gurs, "I began to draw with people milling around me in the barracks. There was no place else where I could work."

Zoran Music wrote:

> I was in a febrile grip. Tomorrow may be too late. For me, life and death depended on these sheets. But will these drawings ever be seen? Will I get out of here alive? We knew that it had been decided to destroy the camp including us, with the explosives at the moment of the retreat of the SS.

Janina Tollik   Ravensbruck Camp (1944)
Pencil drawing 3″ × 4″
Courtesy Janina Jaworska

Alfred Kantor
From the Notebook of Alfred Kantor (1945)
Watercolor, 4″ × 7″
Courtesy Alfred Kantor

Leo Haas   "Slave Labor," Terezin Camp (1943)
Grease pencil drawing, 20″ × 26″
Courtesy Leo Haas

Although most of the artists did secret work alone, in seclusion, some of those who worked together in various studio arrangements conspired as a group to do drawings as messages. This is true of Franciszek Targosz, Mieczyslaw Koscelniak, and Bronislaw Czech in Auschwitz, the artists responsible for salvaging their works and the works of the other artists in the studio by hiding them. These works are now in the Auschwitz Memorial Collection. In Terezin, Felix Bloch, Otto Ungar, Bedrich Fritta, and Leo Haas did the same thing. As Leo Haas recalled, "the Nazis at any moment could decide it was our turn to go, so we had ideas about getting messages out to the world in the event none of us survived."

The artists at the Kovno Ghetto were aided by the Jewish Council:

> To record the repeated atrocities and great suffering inflicted upon our people. It was our duty to record, in every way possible, the horror brought by the Nazis. We worked to preserve Kovno's hour of terror so that future generations would know what had happened and honor the memory of those men, women, and children who suffered the extremes of human misery. We had no camera but we had a highly skilled artist, Esther Lurie, and a young and promising art student Nolick [Benzion Josef Schmidt], for the written word was not enough. Without graphic representation the true sorrow of life struggling under the Nazi domination could not be fully documented.

Brief Profiles

Before the war, the criss-crossing of borders brought many artists to the art centers of Europe from all over the continent, Russia, and Israel (then Palestine). Intermingled with the new directions, all brought their own particular visions and ethnicity which they could not escape. Many became involved in the contemporary art schools and varied movements of their time: *l'Ecole de Paris*, the German Expressionism, *Die Breucke* and *Blaue Reiter*, the *Sezession* movement in Germany, Surrealism, Dada, and the Abstract movement sweeping Europe, as well as others such as the Independents and the *Stzuka*.

The imprisoned artists came from diverse social, economic, and geographic backgrounds. There were Poles, Slovakians, Greeks, Belgians, French, Italians, Germans, Austrians, Armenians, Dutch, Ukrainians, and Danes. They came from every part of the social spectrum: the small towns and villages (*shtetlach*), as well as the great cities, from the most orthodox families to the most assimilated and sophisticated circles of their native lands. They were rich and they were poor. They were trained in art schools in their own countries and abroad. They were killed because they were Jews.

This diversity is reflected in the following brief profiles of a few of the artists, most of whom perished. The list reads like a litany.

Germany and Austria

Felix Nussbaum of Osnabruck, Germany, a promising young artist and winner of many awards, had gained wide recognition by the time he was arrested and sent, along with his wife, to Gurs Camp. They both perished in Auschwitz in 1944. But a number of his works produced in the camp survive him. In 1971, the Osnabruck Museum posthumously honored him in an exhibition of 117 of his paintings. The introduction to the exhibit catalog reads: "In order not only to rediscover an artist who under normal circumstances undoubtedly would have played a major role in the history of German painting but at the same time to make good for the wrong inflicted on the Jewish citizens of Osnabruck as everywhere in Germany in the name of inhuman ideology."[8]

Otto Freundlich was born in Stolp, Pomerania in 1878, studied in Hamburg, Munich, Berlin, and Florence, and settled in Paris. The son of a well-to-do family, he was active in the Sezession and Dada movements and was an early and strong proponent of the abstract art movement in Europe. A well-known and respected intellectual, friend of and co-exhibitor with Picasso, Braque, Mondrian, Signac, Klee, and Groppius, many of whom interceded in his behalf when his work was denounced as degenerate and much of it destroyed by the Nazis.[9] He tried to get his friends, such as Robert Delauney and his wife, to help save the Jewish wives and children. He himself was eventually arrested in Paris and sent to Gurs, Drancy, and then Maidanek,[10] where he was killed on March 9, 1943.

Robert Hanf, born in Germany in 1894, a member of the *Blaue Reiter* and *Die Breuck* schools of art and a friend of Franz Kafka, was active in the Dutch resistance. He was sent on the last train from Holland to Auschwitz.

The daughter of a well-to-do family, Amalie Seckbach was born in Frankfurt in 1899 and had studied in the finest schools in Europe. Sent to Terezin, she perished there in 1943. Some of her works remain.

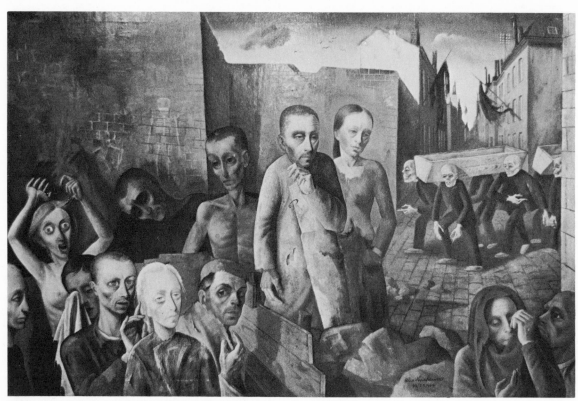

Felix Nussbaum "The Condemned" (1944)
Painting, 25″ × 38″
Courtesy Osnabruck Museum

Rudolf Levy, born on July 15, 1875 in Stettin, Germany, and educated in Paris and Munich, was one of the artists whose work the Nazis listed as degenerate. He lived in Ischia, Italy and was arrested by the SS in Florence on December 12, 1943. Imprisoned in Murate and Capri, he was deported in January 1944 to Dachau where he perished.

Irene Awret was born in Berlin and studied at the Brussels Academy of Fine Arts. Some of her most sensitive drawings were done in Malines concentration camp in Belgium. She managed to save her own works and those of her husband, Azriel.

Felix Bloch was born in Vienna around 1915 and sent to Terezin where he worked with Leo Haas and others in the *Zeichenstube*. He was tortured and killed in 1944 in the Kleine Festung.

Eastern Europe

Esther Lurie, born in Liepaja, Latvia and educated in fine schools in Europe, had emigrated with her family to Palestine. On a visit to relatives in Kovno in 1939, she was seized and arrested by the Nazis. A stage designer as well as a painter, she speaks seven languages. After liberation, she was asked to be an interpreter for the allied forces because she was one of the very few who could speak Russian.

Alexander Bogen was born, lived, educated, taught, and fought in Vilna, Lithuania.

Rachel Szalit-Marcus was born in 1894 to a poor family in Lodz, Lithuania. Wife of the Jewish actor, Julius Szalit, she illustrated the works of Shalom Aleichem, Henri Heine, and Martin Buber's Hassidic stories. Deported in 1942, she perished.

Leopold (Zinajew) Bernstein-Synayeff, born in 1807 in Vilna of an Orthodox Jewish family, was a pupil of Auguste Rodin. Winner of many awards, he did busts of the pope, Cardinal Rampella and other world celebrities. Some of his sculptures were denounced by the Nazis as degenerate art and destroyed in France. Sent to Drancy, he died in one of the death camps.

Osias Hofstatter, gentle philosopher-scholar and artist, born in Poland, began drawing seriously in the camps, encouraged by Karl Schweisig in Gurs. He is today one of Israel's most highly regarded artists and was awarded the coveted Dizengoff Award in 1976, the highest honor Israel bestows on its artists.

George Asher, born in Warsaw in 1894, studied in Paris and was sent to Gurs. His cousin was the noted Polish artist, Roman Kramsztyk, who perished in the Warsaw Ghetto.

Fischel Zber, born in Plock, Poland, on June 23, 1909, was a master graphic artist. In 1936 he went to Paris where he was arrested in 1941 and sent to Beaune-la-Rolande camp. He perished in Auschwitz in 1942.

Russia

Aizik Feder, born in Odessa on July 15, 1887, fled from Russia to Berlin at the age of nineteen, then to Geneva, and finally to Paris. He studied for two years with Henri Matisse. A highly respected artist and member of the *Ecole de Paris* and also of the group referred to as the Jewish School of Paris, he knew Modigliani, Soutine, and Lipchitz. Many of the drawings that he did in Drancy Camp, to which he was sent, survive him. He died in Auschwitz in 1943.

Jaques Gotko was also born in Odessa, in 1900. He studied at the Ecole des Beaux Arts in Paris and did his last works in Drancy and Compiegne.

Erna (Dem) Wolfson was born in 1899 of a wealthy Kiev family whose home was frequented by such people as Sholem Asch and the poet, Hazim Bialik. She studied in Paris and Munich, was a sculptor, ceramist, and painter. Arrested in Paris on July 17, 1942, she perished.

David Brainin was born in Kharkov in 1905. A choreographer, set designer, and portraitist, he was sent to Compiegne and then to Drancy in June 5, 1942, and perished in Auschwitz soon thereafter. Among his surviving portraits is that of Yuri Mandesztam, the son-in-law of Igor Stravinsky.

The Mediterranean Lands

Arturo Levy was born in Trieste on December 17, 1891. An exhibitor in Venice Biennials of 1928, 1930, 1932, he was excluded thereafter. He was sent to confinement in a small village in the province of Le Marche, in central Italy, and then deported to Bergen-Belsen where the allies found him too late to save him from dying of starvation. His works were posthumously included in the Venice Biennial of 1948.

Aldo Carpi lived in Milan and was sent in 1944 to Gusen where he did many drawings and wrote his diary.

Zoran Music was born in the small town of Garizia on the troubled Italy-Yugoslavia border. Multilingual, he studied in Zagreb, and lived and worked in Venice where he was arrested in 1943, and sent to Dachau.

Aizik Feder   "Self-Portrait," Drancy Camp (1943)
Charcoal/pastel drawing, 18″ × 13¼″
Courtesy Biet Lohamei Haghetaot

Yehuda Cohen studied at the Bezalel School in Jerusalem and was born on January 19, 1897, in Salonika, Greece, of a poor artisan family. He traveled widely throughout Europe and was captured on November 7, 1942 in Paris. Sent to Drancy, he perished four days later at one of the death camps.

Other Countries

Rilik Audrieux was a relative of the poet, Rainer Maria Rilke, and was imprisoned in Gurs.

Violette Lecoq was interned in Ravensbruck, the women's hell, where she did gripping drawings of the women prisoners.

Leon Landau of Antwerp was a prominent painter and stage designer for the Royal Theatre. He was incarcerated in Malines, Auschwitz, and perished in Bergen-Belsen.

Jo Spier of Holland was born in 1900 and did some of the most delicate and sensitive drawings while he was imprisoned in Terezin.

Josef Gosschalk, who was born in Zwolle, the Netherlands, on May 12, 1875, did drawings and portraits in Westerbork Camp in Assen, Holland near the German border.

Max van Dam, born in 1910 in Winterswijk, Holland, was a member of the Independents and had exhibited with them in the Stedelijk Museum in Amsterdam, as well as in Venice and Barcelona. He perished in 1943–1944 in Sobibor death camp.

Slavko Bril, noted Yugoslavian sculptor, had studied in Belgrade and was commissioned to do monumental works in Vienna, Paris, and Zagreb. He was murdered by the *Ustachi* (the Croatian Nazis Militia) at Jasenovac death camp[11] in Yugoslavia.

Arnold Daghani did his secret work in a guard's room in Transnistria, the notorious camp in Romania.

Bertalan Gondor, born in 1908 in Budapest, studied art in Vienna and had illustrated the works of Villon and Oscar Wilde before he was sent to the labor camp at Volocz, in the Bereg Province in the Carpathian region of Hungary. Deported to Mauthausen, he perished there in 1944.

Most of the artists incarcerated in Terezin before transfer to the death camps were Czech Jews.

Otto Ungar was born in Husovie, Moravia, on November 27, 1901 and was a beloved art teacher from Brno.

Bedrich Fritta (née Taussig), a well-known illustrator and artist, was born in Ivancice, Moravia on September 9, 1906, incarcerated in 1941; he perished in Auschwitz in 1944.

Karel Fleischmann was born in Klatovy, Bohemia in 1891 and was an esteemed doctor and lover of the arts.

Leo Haas, educated in Germany and France and involved in an interchange of the arts with other countries, was a noted lithographer in Prague.

Malvina Schalkova was born in Prague but studied and lived in her beloved Vienna, her adopted city, until she was captured and sent to Terezin where she died.

Peter Loewenstein was born on January 11, 1919 in Karlsbad, Czechoslovakia. His education as an engineering student at the Charles University in Prague was cut short in the autumn of 1941 when he was sent in the first transport to Terezin. A gifted young man, in 1944 he was sent to Auschwitz, where he perished.

The young art students, Dinah Gottliebova, Alfred Kantor, Adolf Aussenberg and Petr Kien, were sent to Terezin. Suffering from a grave heart disease, Adolf Aussenberg left a series of drawings, mainly of the infirmary where he spent most of his time before he was sent on the "transport east" to perish in Auschwitz in 1944. He also left works that reveal his meanderings into a daydream world.

The brilliant and versatile Petr Kien, born in Varnsdorf, Czechoslovakia on January 1, 1919, displayed his ability early in life. He was sent on the same transport as Fritta to Terezin and continued to study with Fritta while in the camp. Added to his prodigious output of drawings and paintings are short stories and two opera librettos set to music by his friend, Victor Ullman (a student of Arnold Schoenberg), with whom he collaborated at Terezin. The operas are *Die Puppen*, and the recently discovered (1972) *Emperor in Atlantis*, which had its world premiere in 1975 in Amsterdam, was performed in Spoleto in 1976, and had its American debut in San Francisco in 1977. Twenty-five years old in October 1944, Kien was unable to exploit his great potential further because he was sent along with his wife, family, and friend, Victor Ullman, to the gas chambers of Auschwitz where they were all killed.[12]

This is but a short list of the names of artists who were known to have been in the camps. There are, no doubt, hundreds more whose names are still unknown to us. We know some who perished and some whom we are fortunate to have with us still. The amount of work that has survived this gigantic catastrophe makes me marvel, yet in relation to the great numbers who died, and in light of an awareness of the minimum output of a single creative artist, the quantity of works actually seems pitifully small.

Gifts from the Young

There are samples of works by younger prisoners who showed gift and promise.

Peter Ginz was fifteen when he was in Terezin. Too old to be with the children's unit and too young to be with the adults, the thirteen-to-fifteen-year-olds, some dozens of them, were put together. They formed a secret group which they called "Skid." Meeting in Number One, Lager 417, every Friday from December of 1942 until the autumn of 1944, they published a newsletter, *Vedem* ("We're Leading"), of which young Peter Ginz was the editor. There are almost 800 pages of this little paper in the archives of the Terezin Memorial Museum thanks to Zdenek Taussig, the only boy who survived Number One. When the young boys were sent to the gas chamber, the magazine put together in strictest privacy was entrusted to Zdenek Taussig, who wrote that "The magazine was hidden in the forge behind the Magedeburg Barracks where a coal-shed changed into a bedroom was where I slept with my father who was the blacksmith. It was I who brought our magazine from Terezin to Prague." After the liberation, he gave the magazines to two other young authors who had contributed to it, Jiri Kotouc and Zdenek Ornest, who gave the works to the Terezin Memorial Museum. Young Peter Ginz also wrote poetry and made many drawings which also survive him and are in the archives in Yad Vashem in Jerusalem as well as at Terezin. He perished in Auschwitz in 1944 with most of the other boys.[13]

Young "Nolick," Benzion Yosef Schmidt, pictorial archivist of the Kovno Ghetto, was also fifteen years old. He left behind a series of very fine drawings which were salvaged with the archives of the ghetto and are in Israel today. Young Nolick refused to surrender to the order of the Gestapo and leave his bunker despite their threats to blow it up. Nolick perished when his bunker was bombed, but his works have been salvaged and survive him. These are just two of the many young people whose creative potential was crushed in the flower of their youth.

Bohumil Lonek   Terezin (1944)
Pen and ink drawing
Courtesy Terezin Memorial Museum

Petr Kien   "Women Peeling Potatoes," Terezin Camp (1943)
Watercolor, 8″ × 10″
Courtesy Yad Vashem Memorial Museum

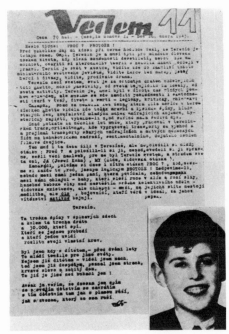

Peter Ginz   Portion of periodical "We're Leading," with photo of P. Ginz, Terezin Camp
Clandestine newspaper, 2/26/43
Courtesy Terezin Memorial Museum

A Caveat from the Children

The expressions of children on paper, with words, in the make-believe of theatre, and in music are different from the work of mature artists and have their own special place in the development of the child. The urge to create in any form is innate in all human beings, and manifests itself early in life. Art is not a gift; the gift is the potential for expression. It is not intended to treat the work of children done in the camps and ghettos in the same context with the adult art, nor should the works be evaluated in the same terms. On the premise, however, that the work found in the camps and ghettos is vital as historical documentation, nothing could be more valid nor more elucidating than the unprejudiced eyes of children as they mirrored their world in their drawings. Meanderings through the use of visual language, these gems are testaments too. Without the ripened intellect of the adult, but with the child's instinct that senses a world gone awry, these are revelations of that strange new world in whose crossfire they were caught, and all the more poignant because these works too were done secretly.

At first glance, there is nothing unusual about these papers. They are very typical of what children do in the various stages of their developing years. The familiar, childlike forms, shapes, and colors are ever present: the huge-head-no-body drawings from which protrude stick-shape arms and legs, by the very small children; the early observation of detail as the children look up into adult faces and draw the up-turned noses — a nostril view — of their world; the splash of blue sky in the upper part of the paper and the stroke of green grass across the bottom of the usual landscapes with the same square houses, the same perpetual daisy flower as big as a tree beside it; and the delightful beginnings of the organization of colors and patterns of the older children. These are all present, no more or less remarkable than other children's statements. Upon closer inspection there is something bizarre about many of the children's works. Amid the familiar appear discomforting elements. Black strokes from odd-sized chimneys dissect the blue and green childscapes. Sometimes an entire page is smudged with a sooty grey. Faces rarely smile and from little eyes flow oversized tears, making an inadvertent pattern over the entire page. The figures of guards with guns, obviously the enemy, loom large over masses of marching people or hover menacingly over the wide-eyed children traumatized with fright in the barrack bunks. Unnatural and oversized forms replace the child who is usually the largest shape in its

Helga Weissova (Hoskova)   "Secret School," Terezin Camp (1943)
(Painted when artist was twelve years old)
Courtesy Helga Weissova Hoskova

Child's crayon drawing
Terezin Camp (c.1941–1945)
Courtesy Prague State Jewish Museum

Henri Pieck   "Behind Barbed Wire," Buchenwald Camp
Charcoal drawing
Courtesy Sachsenhausen Memorial Museum

drawings: spiked barbed wire dwarfs the miniature faces peering through it; soup bowls held by outstretched tiny hands are almost as large as the little figures. There are drawings of children improvising their own playground from available flotsam and jetsam of Terezin Camp; among these the hearse is most common. The subject matter of many of the children's renderings includes people being carried in stretchers, piles of recumbent human forms in the streets, figures being shot or hanging from gallows, and at times randomly placed the *Mogen David* with "Jude" written in its center.

To heighten the poignancy of these messages, the children even signed their names to their papers. Some used initials, some included dates and the word, "Terezin," and in that sweet abandon of the younger child who has just discovered the marks put together have meaning, the first name appears in that universal beginner's scrawl.

Interspersed among the children's works are those that reflect happier times, a kind of remembrance of things past as well as those pieces that depict flights into a world of fantasy. The largest collection of the children's works is in the Prague State Jewish Museum, and instrumental in their preservation were teachers such as Bedriska Brandejsova, who dedicated her last days to distracting the children by giving them secret lessons in art. Like Dr. Janusz Korczak, she perished with them when they were sent to Auschwitz.

Of the fifteen thousand children who passed through Terezin, a meagre one hundred survived. Among them were Yehuda Bacon and Helga Weissova-Hoskova, whose works are among those preserved along with the other children's pieces in Terezin. Yehuda Bacon lives today in Israel and is an artist and teacher. (He testified for Gideon Hausner at the trial of Eichmann about the revolt in Auschwitz which he witnessed.)[14] Helga Hoskova is a painter living in Prague. She writes: "I drew as a child of 12–14 age in Terezin. After my deportation to Osvetim [Czech for Auschwitz], they were hidden and saved by my uncle, some one hundred of them. I was asked many times to sell them but they are of too great a value to me."

Artists in Hiding

Some artists, having gone into hiding, were never deported to the camps. Some were tragically caught. Others managed to hide but conditions were so unbearable that they perished. One such artist was Charlotte Salomon. Born in Berlin in 1917, she fled to France in January of 1939. At some time during this period, while in hiding, she painted her autobiography, which contains over 850 numbered watercolors. She called this series *Das Leben oder Theater* ("All the World's a Stage"), and compared it to a film scenario depicting each event as a separate sequence, with its own type of composition and color scheme. Some scholars have referred to her diary as a counterpart of Anne Frank's diary. She was sheltered for a time by an American widow, Mrs. Ottilie Moore, in Villefranche, France. But the Nazis caught her in 1943, sent her to Gurs, and later deported her to a death camp, possibly Auschwitz.[15]

Chaim Soutine, a recognized modern master, along with Picasso, Braque, Matisse, and Chagall of the *Ecole de Paris*, fled from Paris to the Touraine region of France at the Nazi occupation of that city. He had been offered sanctuary in the United States but refused to emigrate. Born in 1884 to an indigent family, the tenth of eleven children, in the poor and obscure village of Smilowitchi, he was always of delicate health. Developing an intestinal infection, he became deathly ill. Friends found him and took him back to Paris for surgery, but it was too late to save his life.

Tragically aware of the fate of the Jews, in 1941 Marc Chagall accepted the invitation of the Museum of Modern Art to come to the United States, where he remained until 1947, when he returned to France.

Marceli Slodki had an extensive education in art. Born in Lodz, he had studied in Germany and Italy and had been involved in the Dada movement. During the Nazi occupation of Paris, he went into hiding in the mountains. He, too, was caught in 1943 and deported to one of the death camps.[16]

The Desperate Solution

For some artists, life under these conditions was so unbearable that they took their own lives. Born in 1880 near Prague, George Kars studied art in Munich, Madrid, and Paris. A member of the *Ecole de Paris*, he was a friend of Pascin, Utrillo, and Suzanne Veladon with whom he was often seen. Distraught over the news that his entire family was killed in Auschwitz, and unable to bear the loss, he committed suicide on February 5, 1945.

Raphael Schwartz was born in 1874 in Kiev. A painter and sculptor, he had attended the Ecole des Beaux Arts and married a descendant of the French aristocracy. A distinguished artist, he had received the Order of the Legion d'Honneur and was a friend of French celebrities. In 1921 he published a volume of portraits of some of these friends: Gide, Debussy, Rodin, Poincaré. The volume was prefaced by Anatole France. Like many artists, he chose to remain in Paris during its occupation. When he knew that the Nazis were coming to arrest him, he hanged himself in his flat in August 1942. He was sixty-eight years old and wore the yellow star still on his clothes.

The painter Franka Rubinlicht was born in Warsaw to a family of artists. Her sister, Natalia Landau, was a painter who perished in Bialystok. Her brother, Fiszl Rubinlicht, a sculptor, was fatally wounded in the bombing of Warsaw. Another sister, a ballerina in a Vilna Troupe and a brother who was a poet, survived. Franka, however, committed suicide in the Warsaw Ghetto.

Artists of the Resistance

A few of the artists died as members of the resistance and underground groups, whether in action or by Nazi execution. Paul Ullman was born in 1906 in Paris, the son of American parents who made their home in Paris. His father was a painter and his mother a writer. Active in the French underground, he was gravely wounded and captured. He was executed on August 24, 1944.

Jules Gordon, a painter, was born in Siberia. After the Russian revolution, his family moved to Paris, and during World War II he joined the underground and helped to rescue Jewish children at the Swiss-French border. After a fierce battle with the Nazis in the mountains of Grenoble, he was caught, tortured, and executed.

Izak Kreczanowski was born in 1910 in Dobrzyn, Lithuania, and studied at the Warsaw Academy of Fine Arts, and exhibited extensively. In 1941, he was one of a group of Jews taken outside the city of Bialystok and executed in a grove.

The New Humanism

Coming from such diversity, the works naturally cover a wide range of interpretations from the most simple and unsophisticated to the most accomplished statements. As personalized and particularized as the works are, however, those recording the camp life all bear a distinct similarity. "The artists themselves were not members of a single generation, artistic tradition, or ethnic culture. The works

Maria Hiszpanska-Neuman
Ravensbruck Camp (1944)
Pen and ink drawing, 4″ × 5″
Courtesy Janina Jaworska

Mieczyslaw Koscielniak
"Starvation," Auschwitz Camp (1943)
Pen and ink drawing, 6½″ × 5″
Courtesy Auschwitz Memorial Museum

Jacques Ochs   "Entrance to Fort Breendonk,"
Fort Breendonk (1941)
Charcoal drawing
Courtesy Paul Levy, Fort Breendonk Memorial Museum

were conceived and executed in places where imminent death, extreme brutality, malnutrition, emotional and artistic deprivation were considered normal. This accounts for the similarity of subject matter."[17]

In truth, the works need no one to describe or to explain them. Nonetheless, the magnitude of the overwhelming calamity exposed in this art cannot be felt unless the works are viewed in groups. Then, the enormity of the event is shattering. It is like watching a slow-motion film done in funereal cadence as the pictures unravel scene after scene of a macabre and grotesque perverted evil against human beings. These can't be real, they must be surreal meanderings, yet there are so many works by different individuals from so many diverse sections of that ravaged continent. How could so many imagine the same terrible things? The jarring realization is that these pictures do not lie. No one will misunderstand these.

The deathscapes of Alfred Kantor, Felix Bloch, Leo Haas, and Bedrich Fritta, the St. Cyprien scenes of Osias Hofstatter bear each artist's individual imprint but also collectively convey the vastness of the desolation and hopelessness of camp life. The works of Otto Ungar and Jacques Ochs show the bleakness of the barrack world in the monotony and emptiness of rows upon rows of identical buildings made more grim against the background of a brooding, physical world. Frigid exteriors of the camps bear an eerie similarity to the barren interiors of the barracks. They are alike, yet, they are out of line — out of focus — they do not synchronize. One hardly sees more than a tree in many of these barrenscapes. And where there is a tree, it has no leaves. There must have been flowers, and grass, and birds, here — *some* sign of life. Yet even nature seems to shrink from these vales of death. The crematorium churning out its human ash and sending smoke heavenward through the ominous stacks have other symbolic meaning: fear and foreboding for many. They recur in many drawings, as does the barbed wire that twists and turns its treacherous delicacy through the miniature gems of Karl Schwesig's stamps and Kien's drawings of Terezin. Many prisoners found the resolution to their suffering by flinging themselves on the electrified links. The drawings of pits gape like bottomless gorges but they are full of the once-living.

The human form so vital to humanistic art is scarcely recognizable, and unlike any seen in so many works of one period by so many, so consistently. Form and shape are irrelevant terms here. A new, yet uninvented language must be developed to describe this.

Where is the flesh on these bodies? Indeed, these are excellent studies of bone structure. For students of osteology, these are the works to see. There is no muscle, there is no flesh. There is only flaccid hanging skin over bones. The skulls are too large for the shrunken frames. "One has only to compare the withered human form here with, say, Michelangelo's splendid statue of David to recognize what the Holocaust has done to the Renaissance image of man."[18]

Everything sags; the stroke is down in all the works. There are no smiles, everything merges and blends in the pulsating tenor of lugubrious despair. The eyes sink into the skull yet bulge pitifully in the darkened sockets. They are stilled-life in the wasting bodies. The dulled and glazed stare of the *Musselmen* bear no sign of the soul which purportedly rests in every human temple. Stunned and piercing are these eyes, reflecting the horror they see and know, and mirroring for us what we cannot see.

Nonetheless the works of many artists catch some clues of life. Halina Olomucki's nervous lines portray the terror and fear of the women and children. Felix Nussbaum shows in his excellent works the prisoners with penetrating and wondering eyes. The Durerlike drawings of Bucanek in Terezin reveal the pain the eyes beheld, as do so many other works, such as the portraits of Auschwitz prisoners by Franciszek Jazwiecki.

The single forms recumbent in death do not have the peace that is typical of that last repose. Zoran Music's corpses and Aldo Carpi's victims and Bohumil Lonek's linear figures lack the tranquility of death. This "sleep of prisoners" is restive and anguished. The figures are shadows of people who never recovered from the last agony. The atrophy of the human body does not even permit the identification of age or sex. These remnants look ageless and yet old. The common denominator, the great equalizer, here is not death, it is the slow dissolution of the living human form.

The drawings of people herded into groups look like teeming beehives. There is no respite from congestion, no relief from the surrounding misery, no air in this suffocating atmosphere, no solitude in which to die; death comes in heaps. Humanity is compressed in huddles, in bunks, in barracks, in work gangs, in the gas chambers, in the crematoria, in the pits, in coffins. The masses of prisoners marching in transports or stacked away in attics in Terezin are dramatically portrayed in Karel Fleischmann's and Felix Bloch's works. Masses of people standing at exhaustive roll call—in line for food, in line for work, in line to die—are disturbingly felt in the works of Jozef Szajna, George Lielezinski, Boris Taslitsky, and

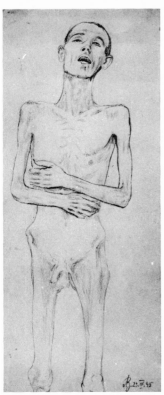

Alois Bucanek   Terezin (1945)
Pencil drawing, 1⅞ ″ × 4 ″
Courtesy Terezin Memorial Museum

Franciszek Jazwiecki   "Portrait of Italian Prisoner,
Davilo Pizzignacco," Auschwitz Camp (1944)
Pencil, 5 ″ × 3½ ″
Courtesy Buchenwald Memorial Museum

Franciszek Jazwiecki
"Self-Portrait," Auschwitz Camp (1944)
Pencil/crayon drawing, 3½ ″ × 5 ″
Courtesy Buchenwald Memorial Museum

Violette Le Coq   Ravensbruck Camp (1945)
Pen and ink drawing, 9″ × 13″
Courtesy Centre de Documentation Juive Contemporaine

Bedrich Fritta   "The Old and the Ill," Terezin Camp (1943)
Pen and ink, 18″ × 25″
Courtesy Thomas Fritta Haas

Leo Haas   Terezin Camp (1943)
Litho pencil drawing, 10″ × 14″
Courtesy Leo Haas

Ota Matousek   Flossenburg Camp (1943–1945)
Wash drawing
Courtesy Sachsenhausen Memorial Museum

Mieczyslaw Koscielniak. Even the ill and dying in Adolf Aussenberg's drawings of the infirmaries were crammed into the too-few cots, and Petr Kien's women in Terezin square sit huddled as they peel potatoes.

Lawrence Langer states so eloquently: "We look at sketches of starving Jews, of crowds waiting to be deported to death camps, of desolate children . . . and we search for terms other than 'beauty' or 'form' to describe what no pen or brush should ever have been inspired to commit to paper or canvas."[19]

People, of course, still sacrifice and work and die for beliefs, but the cause of the Holocaust artists was so strong that it superseded their own safety. This art was created by design not by accident. It was not done to pass time for there was no time in that world. It was not therapy; there was no time for such pampered luxury. It is a deliberate and a desperate art, conceived in agony and suffering and fear and hope. It is truth unveiled in the bits of papers that the artists left behind. The artists did not have to do this work; it was emotionally and physically draining. These on-the-spot reporters daringly sketched an inhuman condition in split-second time as the horrendous scenes unfolded before them.

The selective eye and the touch of the artists, the feeling and spirit so essential to humanistic art, are ever present in these works. Foreboding, discomforting, heart-rending yet elegiac and majestic, one is hushed when viewing this art, feeling oneself to be on sacred ground. It is a revelation of the life and death struggle in the last moments and we are the uncomfortable witnesses of these elegies in form and shape. Even the most sparing of designs reveals much in the little rendered. Looking at this art is not comfortable; it is meant to arouse the conscience and inflame some decent human outrage and indignation.

During the high Renaissance, Leonardo da Vinci wrote:

And you, O man, if you think it would be a criminal thing to destroy this, her work, reflect how much more criminal it is to take the life of a man: and if this, his external form, appears to you marvellously constructed, remember that it is nothing in comparison with the soul that dwells in this structure; for that, be what it may, is a thing divine.[20]

Sara Gliksman-Faitlowitz "The Bridge," Lodz Ghetto (1943)
Oil, 16″ × 20″
Courtesy Jewish Historical Institute

In the Lodz Ghetto my assignment was to work with the other artists in the Statistics Department. One day I was doing my own drawing in pencil instead of the assigned work on the plates. The manager of our department looked over my shoulder and saw it. Fearing the worse, he instead asked me what I would call it. I told him "Expulsion to the Ghetto." After he saw this sketch he brought me paints and other materials I needed to work, and told me to take as much time as I wanted to do the regular assignments. But the hunger was so great, I at times could not sit at my table and work.

Sara Gliksman Faitlovitz
Tel Aviv, Israel, June 1979

4

Art in the Ghettos

The concept of ghettos was not new to twentieth-century Europe. The first recorded pogrom occurred in 38 C.E., and the first ghetto established around 140 C.E. when the Jews of Rome were forced to live in "communities." In 1555 Pope Paul IV built a wall around this community and it became the first enclosed ghetto. Jews who did not already live within the enclosure were compelled to move there. The gates were locked at dusk and reopened at dawn. Any Jews found outside the wall after the closing of the gate were punished. Nonetheless, the Jews of Rome survived the crumbling Roman Empire, the death of Caesar, who had befriended them, the triumph of Titus, the Crusades, anti-Jewish legislation, and the vicissitudes and vagaries of papal ambiguity. This sequestering of the Jews lasted until the *Risorgimento*, the unification of Italy in 1870, at which time the walls around the ghetto were torn down and the emancipation of the Jews was proclaimed.[1]

Ghettos in Europe 1939–1945

The establishment of ghettos under Nazi rule was the machination of Reinhard Heydrich. Eichmann so impressed Heydrich with the success of his Office of Immigration in Vienna that he gave Eichmann the signal to begin the confinement of Jews.[2] The Nazi goal in establishing these ghettos was more insidious than any before

89

this time. The cobweb structure of the ghetto system far surpassed their earlier models. They were set up as way stations and collection centers to the death camps and for the destruction of European Jewry. The Nazis devised their own special methods for killing and murder in the ghetto, methods called *Aktions* and such others as shootings, or burning down the entire ghetto with the inhabitants inside, as was done to the Janow Ghetto in 1943.[3] Sometimes only parts of a ghetto were burned down. "In the action of September 17, 1941, they burnt the hospital complete with its patients and medical staff," related Esther Lurie. "At the liquidation of the Ghetto, in 1944, it was set on fire from every side, and to prevent the Jews from hiding in the buildings, they were shelled and burnt."[4]

The Nazis' first "experimental" ghetto was a detention center in Nisko, Poland, in 1939. It is to this center that Leo Haas was sent, along with one thousand Jews from Czechoslovakia and another thousand Jews from Vienna in October 1939. "We were the forced labor crews, and were arrested to build the structures for the people who would be coming there as well as for ourselves. While we were working on these *Baracken*, we lived in the open fields until we finished. These buildings accommodated twenty horses or 400 people. When they were built, 2000 of us were crammed into them," Leo explained. While incarcerated here, Leo Haas made pencil portraits of the SS officials.

This ghetto was so successful for the Nazis that it served as the catalyst for the formation of ghettos throughout Europe: the Baltic countries, Latvia, Lithuania and Estonia; Poland, Byelorussia, and the Ukraine. By the autumn of 1941, within two years of the issuance of the directive to form ghettos, the Jews from all over Europe were isolated behind walls, barbed wire, or fences.[5]

The ghettos were located in the worst possible sections of the cities and towns. Warsaw, the largest ghetto of all, was situated in the poorest section of that city as was the ghetto in Lodz. Vilna, the "Little Jerusalem of Lithuania," was set in the center of that city. At times entire villages were turned into ghettos or a "district" was formed by consolidating a larger ghetto with smaller ones (much like the larger camp complexes of Auschwitz, Mauthausen, and Buchenwald and their satellites). Kovno Ghetto, for example had seven distinct labor camps. Completely sealed off, in Warsaw with its impregnable stone wall, and in Lodz with its impenetrable barbed wire and board fence, no one could enter or leave except on work crews or by special pass. No mail was permitted in or out or

Esther Lurie   "Entrance to the Ghetto, Kovno," Kovno Ghetto (1941–1942)
Pen and ink drawing, 6″ × 8″
Courtesy Esther Lurie

any business transactions with the outside world.[6] About Kovno, Esther Lurie comments: "Wooden pillars two metres high with seven barbed wires across the width and three across the length— that was the fence that closed us off from the world. . . . Along the entire fence was a well-armed patrol. Nobody entered or departed without a special permit."

Almost all the ghettos were situated in eastern Europe, and they became surrogate camps as the conditions therein progressively deteriorated. The one major difference between camps and ghettos was that the camp population consisted of political prisoners, prisoners of war, criminals, dissidents, gypsies, and Jews; the ghetto population was entirely Jewish. The same restrictions were imposed, however, and the most basic human needs were denied. Starvation, disease, and congestion prevailed and Jews from all socioeconomic backgrounds were compressed together, adding communication problems to the already insurmountable and insupportable conditions.[7] To one ghetto, for example, Jews from seventy-five different areas were sent. Even those who no longer considered themselves Jews, nonreligious Jews, converts to Christianity (as was the artist, Roman Kramsztyk, who had been baptized), and *Mischlinge* (Jews of mixed marriages) were compelled to live in these enclosures.[8]

Cultural Activities in the Ghettos

The ghettos were actually established as collection centers to facilitate the shipment of Jews to the death and slave labor camps. To carry out the charade that they were established as safeguards for Jews until after the war, to repel problems of rebellion or panic, and for easier control of the masses, cultural and educational activities were permitted in some of the ghettos at the incipient stages of their existence.[9]

Cultural events included theater, revues, symphonies, and other musical and stage performances. Five professional theaters operated in Warsaw Ghetto (two in Yiddish and three in Polish). There was a puppet theater in Lodz. The symphony orchestra in Warsaw was eventually denied the right to perform because it had played music by proscribed "Aryan" composers while, in Vilna Ghetto, three performances a month were held that included the Aryan composers' works. Lodz had its symphony and also stage revues. Art exhibits and art contests were held. In some of the ghettos, these exhibitions were held for exploitative purposes. Chaim Rumkowski, the chief of the Judenrat in Lodz, ordered that art exhibits be held. In Vilna, Jacob Gens, the leader of Vilna's Jewish Council, arranged for art contests. He nominated the jury and approved the candidates for awards, and financed the awards.[10]

In her history on the Holocaust, Nora Levin writes that the Germans permitted the opening of a Graphic School of Art in the Warsaw Ghetto. Courses included engraving, watchmaking, leatherwork, and architectural drawing. Quoting from the diary of sixteen-year-old Mary Berg, she notes that an exhibition was held of pictures showing fruits, flowers, designs for compacts, book covers, posters, signs, and designs for homes. From the diary entry of May 6, 1942, she writes that the graphics instructor took his students to the site of a bombed-out house. The pupils painted a fresco of animal cartoons on one of the walls of the ruined house.

Assigned Art in the Ghettos

The artists who were incarcerated, either permanently or briefly as a stopover to the camps, came from diverse experiences and levels of expertise, as did the artists in the camps. Many of them belonged to important art organizations in their native countries. In Poland, for example, many were members of the *Zachenta* (National Institute for the Promotion of the Plastic Arts). The drive to record despite all the dangers and risks never faltered. Those artists who had to do assignments also did their own secret work.

As in the camps, the professionals, craftsmen, musicians, actors, writers, and artists proved useful to the Nazis. The Judenrat (the Jewish council set up by the Nazis, supposedly to serve as a liaison between the Jewish community and the Nazis) organized workshops, studios, and other departments, as well as issuing individual assignments to meet the unique needs of each community. There were statistics departments in Warsaw, Lodz, Vilna, Kovno, and Czestochowa ghettos where the work assigned to the artists included making charts, diagrams, graphs, and records.

The second largest ghetto was Lodz, the center of the textile industry in Poland, near the Chelmno death camp. There was a graphics department located in an abandoned Catholic church and the artists filled the heavy demand for signs. The counterfeit work forged there produced the bank notes and stamps, like their counterparts in Sachsenhausen concentration camp. In the Scientific Division of Lodz, sculptors carved burlesque figures of eastern European Jews and also designed exhibits of Jewish life for the *Gettoverwaltung* Museum (the Ghetto German Administration).

On March 1, 1941, by order of Rumkowski, the House of Culture was opened in Lodz. A special room was set aside for the artists who were bribed into working with promises of free food stamps. By December 6, 1941, sixty musicians and ten artists were employed. They painted scenery for the revues in the theater and for other stage performances, and painted portraits upon demand by the officials.[11] Rumkowski had many portraits painted to show himself as the patron of the arts as well as a man of the people. One portrait by an artist named H. Szylis, dated 1941, shows him as a father figure looking over the ghetto.[12] Many portraits abound showing Rumkowski standing guard over the sleeping ghetto, spreading his mantle around the starving children.

Posters were also produced.[13] The well-known Polish painter, Szymon Szerman, who was born in Lodz in 1917 and perished there in 1943, was one of twelve artists employed in the statistics department. Some of his works were salvaged and are in the collection of the Biet Lonamei Haghetaot. Another worker in the statistics department in Lodz, Sara Gliksman Faitlovitz, was an established painter and winner of many awards prior to her incarceration. Her assignment was to make records for the statistics department. Said Sara,

> I had to make plates such as showing the ration of food supply to the population. This was so ridiculous for one need only look out the window and see the piles of the dead in the streets and the lines of people waiting for food when there was none, to realize the futility of such records, not to mention the unspeakable hunger we all felt. Rumkowski himself asked me to do some work for him. He was so anxious to be known as a good leader that he had me do fabricated statistics to this end.

Itzak (Vincent) Brauner, who was a native of Lodz, also had to do portraits of Rumkowski. Some of his works of ghetto scenes, and some of his portraits are located in the Polish Historical Institute. He perished in Auschwitz in July of 1944.

The Kovno Ghetto had a *Mal und Zeichen Werkstätte* (a painting and drawing workshop) that made up numerous placards, announcements, diagrams, boards, signs, and symbols and executed all manner of graphics including drawings for the Germans.

In Vilna the Jewish Council subsidized a "Union of Writers and Artists." This became the congregating place of the ghetto's elite. They sponsored art contests and held exhibitions.[14] Besides the work generated by its statistical department, and its Union of Writers and Artists, some of the artists in Vilna were forced to do individual assignments. Jacob Szer, an established painter of Vilna, was forced to do portraits of the Nazi officials. As did so many other artists, he painted scenery for the ghetto's various theater productions and also lectured on art during his imprisonment. He was sent to Vaivari camp where he was killed by the Gestapo.

The Warsaw Ghetto council, whose chief was Avram Chierniakow, employed about twenty musicians, writers, painters, and sculptors in the "Grindstone and Cleaning Workshop" situated at 9 Mila Street. They were required to do all the various graphic work that needed the skillful hand of trained artists.[15] Among the artists who worked in the Grindstone and Cleaning Workshop was Maksymilian Eljowicz, who was born in 1890 near Plock, Poland, a member of the *Zachenta*, and a member of the Jewish Association for the Propagation of Art. Known chiefly as a portraitist, he had exhibited in the Salon d'Automne in Paris. Together with Feliks Futerman, Feliks Fredman (head of the Jewish Artists Organization in Poland), and Simha Trachter, who were also in the workshop, he executed a giant wall painting, "Job," and a fresco at the reception hall of the Judenrat. Another painting ordered by the Germans, "Jews at Work," was maliciously and deliberately destroyed the day after its completion by the very Germans who had commissioned it. All these artists perished in Treblinka during the Action in 1942. With Eljowicz, perished his son and his wife the painter, Stefanja Eljowicz.[16]

The Secret Art in the Ghettos

Prisons can confine bodies but not minds. In the ghettos many took part in clandestine activities, sometimes with the sanction of the councils who looked the other way or whose members became actively involved. Many of the activities that were allowed at first were later forbidden. (This merely meant that the Jews went underground to the bunkers or in other temporarily safe and secluded places.) Classes, poetry readings, lectures, meetings of all types went on in many of the ghettos. Such secret activities in the Warsaw Ghetto bunkers are vividly described in the diary of Emmanuel

Esther Lurie   "Potato Field," Kovno Ghetto (1941)
Pen and ink drawing, 10″ × 12″
Courtesy Esther Lurie

Sara Gliksman-Faitlowitz   "Expulsion," Lodz Ghetto (1943)
Pencil drawing, 4″ × 5″
Courtesy Yad Vashem Memorial Museum

Ringelblum.[17] In March of 1943, at the Cultural House on 6 Strazun Street in Vilna, exhibits were opened at night and disguised during the day. A secret museum was organized in the abandoned buildings showing art, religious and secular books, Torah scrolls, and other religious objects. The artists of the ghettos actively participated in these ventures, fully aware of the great risks they were taking.[18] Like their counterparts in the camps, the artists doing secret work recording the ghetto scenes and ghetto life lived under the constant threat of exposure and punishment. As Leo Haas says of his experience in the ghetto: "We were often in danger and had to use greatest caution in hiding from the SS men who were spread out all over the ghetto." And Esther Lurie recounts:

> Standing in front of the ruins I began to draw. A guard saw me and warned me not to go on. It was clear that I could not continue in the open. I found myself in an attic of an abandoned house. There I completed two sketches without further interference . . . and as the ghetto got emptier and emptier it was not possible for me to work. I did not draw any longer. The SS men who were now living among us interfered everywhere and caused a state of constant tension. . . . I set out to sketch whatever seemed important to me, but it was dangerous to do any sketching in the streets.

In Lodz, Sara Gliksman Faitlovitz

> sought out a place in the ghetto where I could paint secretly and without fear of being discovered. I found such a place in the office of an engineer friend. This office had a window which faced out under the bridge of the ghetto. I asked him if it was not dangerous to paint here, and he said it was safe and secret. No one could come in for the door would be locked. I could paint here whenever I wanted. Even though I painted all the time in my office refuge, the hunger was so great that work did not always assuage the hunger as I had hoped it might. Besides the hardship there was always the risk of getting caught.

Sara painted thirteen works here in secret. The bridge was painted from three different views. One view of the bridge is now in the museum at Yad Vashem, one in the Museum of Martyrology of Warsaw, and the other in the Lodz Museum. Six other works are at Yad Vashem and the rest disappeared. Among the artists in the ghetto were Henoch Barczynksy, who had done a portrait of the distinguished poet Yitzhak Katzenelson, and the artists Maks Haneman, Maurjcy Trembacz, Pola Lindenfeld, and Nathan Spigel, a member of the art organization START. All perished in Lodz.[19]

The Eltestenrat of the Kovno Ghetto not only took great pains to keep secret archives about the occurrences in the ghetto but also encouraged the arts as far as was possible. Avraham Golub-Tory, the deputy secretary of the council, was also a member of the *Matzok*, the ghetto's underground resistance movement. It is he who hid the records in five sets of tin-lined boxes including the drawings of Esther Lurie and young Nolick.[20] Three of these five important cases of information were recovered after the liberation. Mr. Tory also provided a special meeting place in the house of a friend. He described the meetings as

> a literary circle, composed of several writers, poets, historians, and artists, and we met every two weeks. Among us was a journalist and we had a clandestine radio. He would give us a survey on the state of the war by summarizing and bringing to us his analysis. Included in this circle was Dr. Shapiro, a brilliant scholar of Hebrew literature who on the eve of the war had published a monumental book on the history of Hebrew Literature. So this bunch of guys made up our group. We couldn't eat but we could talk. I asked Esther and another artist to make an exhibit for just a few people to be held during the curfew. A small exhibit, but it was so good that I knew that these works were as valuable as any writers. So Esther did also works for the archives recording what was happening in the ghetto. Many more exhibits of Esther's works were held.

Esther Lurie corroborated Mr. Tory's account:

> Mr. Tory asked me to do some drawings as records for the archives. It was very risky but being a member of the underground as well he knew which guards could be bribed and how to get us a "permit." Accompanying Mr. Tory as his wife to get personal belongings from our former home, we walked to the small ghetto which was out of limits for us.

And, Mr. Tory continued,

> After this first expedition Esther and I became a team and we made other visits to places considered important in documenting the story of the ghetto. Admiration for her work spread throughout the ghetto as more and more Jews became aware of her mission.

Other artists worked in Kovno. Jacob Lifschitz was born in Kovno where he and Esther Lurie worked together, as she de-

Benzion Josef Schmidt (Nolick)   "Transport," Kovno Ghetto (1943)
Watercolor, 8″ × 10″
Courtesy Avraham Golub-Tory

Roman Kramsztyk "Jewish Family," Warsaw Ghetto (1943)
Charcoal
Courtesy Jewish Historical Institute

scribes: "On some free days did the painter, Jacob Lifschitz and I sketch ghetto types." He perished in Dachau but his wife and daughter saved his work and took it to Yad Vashem. Sali Beker, another artist, was one of the first victims of the Nazis in Kovno in the action that took place in 1941.

Vilna, the jewel of Jewish culture and thought, the cultural center of Jewish tradition, was actually one of the most highly active ghettos. Among the painters who took part in the clandestine exhibits with Jacob Szer was Schmuel Bak (Samuel Bak) then a youngster, and today an artist in Israel.[21] The first artist-victim of the Germans in Vilna was Natan Korzen. Forced out of his studio, which was burned along with his works, he himself was hanged. Other artists from the Vilna Ghetto whose works have been preserved are Nahum Rombeck, M. Bahelfer, L. Mefgashilski, David Lankovski, and Faival Segal.[22] And in and out of Vilna and the Narocz Forest, aiding the underground and fighting with the resistance and the Jewish Brigade, was Alexander Bogen, who did survive, as did a number of the works that he did at this time.

The famous Polish artist, Roman Kramsztyk, was sent to the Warsaw Ghetto. The son of a wealthy and distinguished family, he had been educated abroad. A member of the *Zachenta* (National Institute for the Promotion of Plastic Arts) in Poland and the *Sezession* movement in Berlin, he was the product of the *Ecole de Paris*. Just before the outbreak of World War I, he exhibited widely in Europe: London, Venice biennials, and Paris, including the "New Sezession Exhibition" in Berlin with Matisse, Renoir, and Max Lieberman. Although he had converted to Christianity, he shared the fate of all the other Jews in the ghetto and was killed in the 1942 action in the ghetto by a soldier of the Vlassov Commandos. Prolific during his imprisonment, those of his works that were salvaged from the ghetto are preserved in the Warsaw Historical Insitute in Poland.

Among the artists in the Warsaw ghetto were Adam Herszaft, a graphic artist who died in Treblinka after his studio was burned down by the Germans, and Regina Mundlak, Izk Perel, Bzszaszinska, and Igo Sym—all of whom perished in the ghetto.[23]

Cracow Ghetto on the Vistula River in Poland near Auschwitz was one of the poorest areas. Abraham Neuman, confined there, was a painter and a member of the *Zachenta*. He continued to paint during the occupation of Cracow. So ill that he could not stand when he was forced from his studio during the action of June

4, 1942, a "Nazi smashed his head with his rifle butt" and killed a friend who was with him—the Yiddish poet, Mordecai Gebertig.[24] When all the ghettos were designated for liquidation in 1943, Cracow Ghetto was destroyed.

It is known that the painter of small genre scenes, life in the villages, and figures of Jewish people, Erno Erb, born in Lwow perished there in 1943, as did the artist, Jacob Glasner, who was killed in one of the actions of 1943.

Liquidation of the Ghettos and the Fate of the Art Works

In 1943 Heydrich called for the liquidation of all the ghettos, and by 1944 it was accomplished.[25] Only the Lodz ghetto was left intact because its production of material was crucial to the Nazi war effort. In the wake of this wanton destruction, most of the ghetto art was destroyed, although some was hidden with the archives or smuggled out to friends and thereby salvaged. (Halina Olomucki's sketches were kept until after the liberation by a friend on the "outside" of the ghetto wall.)

It is ironic that many of the religious artifacts held so sacred by the Jewish communities of the various cities were saved by the Nazis' confiscation. Themselves aware of the existence of the artifacts and treasures and of their monetary value, Einsatzstab Rosenberg, set up by Hitler to ransack the museums and homes of European Jews, also looted and pillaged the priceless and sacred collections of the religious communities now ensconced in the ghettos. In Cracow, one of the oldest of the Jewish communities, many of the religious artifacts and other ceremonial objects were stolen by the brigade. Berson Museum, with its sacred collection of the Warsaw Jewish Community, was forcibly closed. When it reopened a few months later, it was empty and even the glass showcases had been taken. The sacred Goldstein Collection of Lodz and the Gieldinsky Collection in Danzig were all confiscated and taken to Germany.[26] Three hundred and seventy-five archives and 531 educational institutions, 402 museums and 457 libraries were denuded of their precious collections, which were sent to Frankfurt. Those items considered unimportant were burned or shredded for recycling at the paper mills.

Halina Olomucki   "Boy Selling the Star," Warsaw Ghetto (1943)
Charcoal, 7″ × 9″
Courtesy Halina Olomucki

Otto Ungar   "Terezin Barracks"
Gouache, 9" × 12"
Courtesy Terezin Memorial Museum

Photograph of
Terezin Barracks today
(part of Terezin Memorial Museum)
taken by John Costanza, 1979
Collection of the Author

The ever-vigilant scribe of the Warsaw Ghetto, Ringelblum, whose articulate records about life in the ghetto reveal the importance Jews placed on keeping statistics, wrote in his notes:

We must look after the future. In time of massacre such as this, with all of European Jewry being slaughtered, the soul of each and every Jew is precious and we must take pains to try to preserve it. Jews have always adapted themselves to the hardest of times, have always known how to survive the hardest times.[27]

Charlotte Buresova wrote:

I was nearly forty when in Terezin. I would have so much to tell you about art and life in the ghetto camp. This cannot be written in a short time especially from a person who doesn't know your language. Many people like to forget what happened. But I, though I was not damaged, cannot forget. It was terrible but it gave me much confidence and it was a very hard school for my present life. There were many events in those years. First my husband's illness and then my eyes. I was nearly blind for two years, but now, after two operations, I see again. You see I can write and read—and PAINT! So I am happy.[28]

Leo Haas   "Countdown in Terezin," Terezin Camp (1943)
Litho pencil drawing, 18″ × 24″
Courtesy Leo Haas

I *feel it my duty to accuse, until the end of my life, the fascist murderers named in my report, and to accuse the men in the background—in the name of all the victims, in my own name, and above all in the name of my friends who did not return, the painters of Terezin.*

Leo Haas,
The Affair of the
Painters of Terezin

5

Leo Haas' Account of the Artists of Terezin

Terezin might be most suitably used as a ghetto. . . . then the evacuation of the Jews from this temporary concentration camp to eastern territories (where their numbers will already be greatly decimated). . . . Transport to the ghetto of Terezin would not require much time. Two or three trains containing a thousand Jews each could be sent every day. According to the well-tried method, let each Jew take with him luggage up to fifty kilograms in weight and food for from a fortnight up to four weeks, which will make it easier for us. Straw will be allocated to the empty flats in the ghetto, for beds would take up too much room. The larger flats in the good houses may be at the disposal only as official flats for the Zentralstelle in the ghetto, for the Council of Elders, the food commissariat, and especially for the corps of guards. Let the Jews build flats under the earth. . . .[1]

Fifty to sixty thousand Jews can be comfortably accommodated in Terezin. . . . After the complete evacuation of the Jews, Terezin will, according to a perfect plan, be settled by Germans and become a centre of German Life."[2] [Extracts from official records.]

As a result of these orders, the first contingent of 342 Jewish workers and craftsmen were forcibly recruited from the Czech population and sent on November 24, 1941, to prepare the former town of Terezin to become a ghetto camp.[3] Among the young men in this first crew of slave laborers were Peter Loewenstein and Alfred Kantor. Alfred Kantor relates:

> I helped prepare that place from a military post to a settlement for Jews. (The ruse) was that it was in our best interest to go. The Germans used every means of reassurance to foster the delusion that all that was involved was a matter of relocation. . . . The mimeographed orders specified (among other things) to bring enough food for ten days and that we were to be processed which simply meant nothing more than robbing us of whatever valuables we might have. On the fourth day after reporting to a central point we were marched at daybreak all thousand of us to the railroad station a half mile away. . . . A special train awaited us and took us quickly to Terezin. As the train pulled out of the station, I knew we were all captives of the Germans and that our fate was uncertain.[4]

Terezin in Czech, Theresienstadt in German (also referred to as Theresienbad,) the town was founded in 1780 by Emperor Joseph of the Hapsburg family for his mother, the queen, Maria Theresa. Located in the Bohemia section of Czechoslovakia about forty miles north of Prague and two hundred miles west of Auschwitz, it nestles in the fork of the Ohre and Labe rivers, surrounded by the rolling countryside with the haze of the Bohemian Central Mountain range in the distance. The fortress town was built in the shape of an octagonal star bordered on all sides by a high scarped wall and a moat as deep as the wall is high. A baroque town in two sections — the large fortress and the small fortress — the ground plan is symmetrical with many intersecting streets leading into several squares. On the perimeter of the main square in the town are a church and administrative buildings. Blocks of houses and barracks have identical plans with the same number of stairs, gates, and courtyards in each block.

Terezin became a garrison town in 1882. In the twentieth century, its situation, location, and barricaded layout made it a natural and impregnable prison, ideally suited to the Nazis' purposes.

At the remote end of the town was the little fortress, or *Kleine Festung*. A punishment center, it had solitary cells (in one had been incarcerated the assassin of Archduke Ferdinand, Gavrilo Princep, and to this same cell sometime later Leo Haas was sent), a shooting wall, a gallows, a torture chamber, and underground passageways. In this sector were the SS headquarters and staff buildings, the hospital, and other block units. A railroad ran through

Peter Loewenstein   "Ground Plan of Terezin"
Pencil drawing, 7″ × 10″
Courtesy Gerda Korngold

Alfred Kantor
"Two Views of Terezin," Terezin Camp (1941)
Colored pencils, 4″ × 6″
Collection of the Author

Felix Bloch "Transport," Terezin Camp (1941)
Wash drawing, 7″ × 10″
Courtesy Prague State Jewish Museum

Terezin to Auschwitz and in the opposite and distant part of the town from the *Kleine Festung* a crematorium with four ovens was eventually built.[5] A town intended for a maximum population of 7,000 had 60,000 to 70,000 inhabitants during the Nazi occupation.

In the mid-twentieth century, the Germans, considering themselves the successors to the crusaders, again persecuted the Jews under the sign of the swastika as the crusaders had done under the sign of the cross. In fact, Himmler wanted the SS to become the new "Order of the Cross."[6]

Leo Haas' Account

There are several mysteries concerning the discovery of our secret work but I don't think we'll ever know the answer. One account claims that our works were seen in Switzerland after the collector, Frantisek Strauss smuggled them out. However, I think it happened another way. We often traded our works for things we needed, and we may have been betrayed when the works fell into the wrong hands. Fritta was always worried about getting better food for his son, Tommy. He exchanged his sketches for some jam. It is possible this person was the informer.

It is true, however, that after the inspection team left Terezin, investigation began in regard to our work. It was rumored about the camp that the Nazis were not pleased about certain questions these inspectors asked, which indicated they knew more than what was in the SS briefing. After their departure, Fritta, Ungar, Bloch, and I were summoned by Dr. Otto Zucker[7] at the office of the Council of Elders and were told to bring warm clothing in the event we would be detained for questioning. We suspected it was about our art work so we immediately set about to hide it. Without tools but with the help of an engineer friend, we hid four hundred of my works and some of Fritta's in the barrack wall. The rest of Fritta's we buried in a tin case. To avoid suspicion we left a few harmless sketches around to stop the "mouths of the wolves." What surprised and worried us was that there was no house search and no raid on the studio.

In the Kommandant's office we were joined by the architect Norbert Troller and the collector, Frantisek Strauss. After some time in the damp cellar we were hustled into the office of SS captain, Karl Raum, who had with him the "bird of death," SS captain Moes and SS captain Hans Gunther whom I knew from Nisko. One other was present whom

Otto Ungar   "Night Burial," Terezin Camp
Gouache, 9″ × 12″
Courtesy Yad Vashem Memorial Museum

Karel Fleischmann   "Registration," Terezin Camp (1943)
Ink wash drawing, 10″ × 16″
Courtesy Prague State Jewish Museum

I recognized from his visits, Adolph Eichmann. Eichmann began the questioning in soft and unctuous tones expressing how grieved he was by our slanderous representation after all he was trying to do for the Jews. Considering this no minor incident, he wanted to know if we were an organized group forming a communist cell and who was backing us. With a few sketches before him, he turned to me and said, "This Jewish fantasy, distorting the truth, there must be someone behind you." As I look back on it I am amazed at my audacity to draw Eichmann into a discussion on art. I responded, "I see you know a lot about art, and that you must have read a lot about it." He assented, "Yes, yes, so what of it?" "Well," I replied, "you must know the expression, study by nature. What we are doing is not Jewish fantasy but it's drawn from life. It is a life study." He sharply retorted, "You mean to say people here are suffering from hunger?" I answered him, "I'm not saying it, I've drawn it."

Exasperated when their questioning did not produce the desired answers, they sent us back to the cellar until evening when in typical Nazi fashion Gunther and Moes with their guards drove us up the stairs with blows from their rifle butts. In the courtyard canvas-topped vans awaited us. With dismay, in them we saw our families: Fritta's wife and three-year-old son, Tommy, Ungar's wife and five-year-old daughter, my wife and Mrs. Bloch, Troller and the Strausses!

They drove us to the little fortress—the dreaded fortress—where upon arrival we, including the children, were forced to stand facing the wall. Then the women and children were led to solitary confinement, and after a while Fritta and I were separated from Ungar and Bloch. Later I found out that Bloch was killed as a result of the beatings, and that they had mutilated Ungar's working hand so severely that two fingers had to be amputated. They crushed his hand to a pulp so that he could draw no more "lies about them." It was no accident that Fritta and I were not killed; we had to serve as examples to the others.

Sent to work with the slave-labor crews, the interrogation and beatings never stopped. They were so fierce that I became ill and my legs began to swell from the severity of the treatment and I was barely able to walk. This was dangerous for if we couldn't work, we were considered useless and would be killed. The capo in my cell, a Dr. Wurzel and his friend, operated on my leg with a rusty knife and scissors, without sterilization or anesthetics, to save my life. Then they hid me under a pile of rags in the cellar. I was found one day by the yard commander, and placed in solitary confinement in the same cell where the assassin, Princep, had

Bedrich Fritta   Terezin Camp (1943)
Wash drawing, 18″ × 24″
Courtesy Thomas Fritta Haas

been. I was forbidden food or water but my friends found a hole in the wall of that cell and placed water and soup for me there. When the Nazis found me still alive after a month they began to crowd my tiny cell with other prisoners. There were so many of us in there that we could neither sit nor lay. We stood and moved in shifts.[8]

I was eventually served with an indictment, as was Fritta, accusing us of horror propaganda and a warrant for our arrest with *RU* (return not desirable) stamped on it, which meant we would be sent on a transport east. I saw Fritta again when we were preparing to leave on the transport to Auschwitz. The brutal treatment had taken its toll on him. He could no longer walk or talk. I offered to take care of him and they unshackled the chains from our hands and feet. He was a head taller than I but I propped him against my back and dragged him along with me. His suffering was so great that when we arrived in Auschwitz so broken in mind and body, Fritta lost consciousness and died a few days later.

After the liberation I returned to Terezin and found that my wife and all the members of the artists' families had remained in solitary confinement during that time. The women and children had slept on the earthen floor of their cells. Mrs. Ungar and her daughter were alive, as were my wife and little Tommy Fritta. Hansi, Fritta's wife, however, had died. My wife, who had become an invalid as a result of her experiences there, and I adopted Tommy Fritta as our son. She lived only ten years after her liberation. At that time it was 1955, I was offered a post as political cartoonist for *Eulenspiegel* Magazine in East Berlin, which I accepted.

Not one of the artists revealed the places where our works were hidden. Not with all the beatings and the torture did we tell. I found all the work we had so desperately hidden, intact, when I returned to Terezin in that year of 1945.[9]

Esther Lurie   Leibitz Camp (1944)
Drawing on back of cotton paper wrapping, 4″ × 6″
Courtesy Esther Lurie

In Leibitz women's labor camp, I could not spend much time at it [drawing], for I had to be careful not to be seen. . . . I succeeded in completing only a small number of sketches much as I longed to record on paper all that I saw. We looked pitiful. 1,200 Jewish women put to work on fortifications and slept in tents. . . . Carrying heavy shovels we were marched off every morning for several miles escorted by armed SS guards. Hardly anyone had anything to wear except rags. Many were barefoot— frostbite was a common ailment among the women. On our left sleeve we wore the patch with the star of David, and our camp number. About fifty young girls aged nine to fifteen were also with us. Their mothers had concealed their ages, and the little girls could hardly keep up with us. Their mothers carried their shovels for them and it was touching to see these little girls' efforts to appear grown-up. I wanted to draw all this but it was dangerous and difficult, now. . . . I did drawings which I hid in my clothes where they remained for months.

Esther Lurie
Artist-survivor
Tel Aviv, Israel, June 1979

6

Charcoal, Woodchips, Paper Shreds:
The Media of Camps and Ghettos

Compounding the problems for the artists was the lack of materials. To begin with, those that the Nazis gave them or those found were usually of inferior quality. None of the works seen up to this time was created with materials of fine quality. Nonetheless, those working on assigned projects could avail themselves of some supplies. In other camps artists would try to bribe the guards to mail letters requesting supplies and smuggle in the packages when they did arrive at the camps.

Leo Haas tells of the imprisoned wealthy Czech collector, Frantisek Strauss, who had Christian contacts through marriage on the outside, and had such things as food, cigarettes, money, and other precious items smuggled into Terezin. With these he purchased the artists' works and expanded his collection. Some of the works he kept in the barracks, some he hid; some, however, he smuggled out of the camp via his friends.

Early in the war, organizations, relief agencies, were able to send supplies to the prisoners. At Terezin, the artists were initially permitted to bring along art supplies when they were sent there. This is probably why so many watercolors and oils were done in this camp, but such supplies were never replenished when exhausted.

The artists who did not work on special assignments or were sent to camps where restrictions were so great that no contact with the outside world was possible had the most difficult time of all.

117

The search for materials was complicated by the fact that all materials had to be hidden until they could be put to use. In all cases the ingenuity of the artists knew no bounds, nor did their daring.

As the Germans felt their imminent defeat, they imposed even more stringent restrictions and deprivations on inmates. Only work crews continued to build and work in the munitions plants, quarries, and factories. No more packages were delivered; all outside sources and contacts were cut off. Mail—or what there was of it— was stopped, and more and more Jews, including the artists and the collectors, were sent in the acceleration of transports to the extermination centers. (The collector Strauss and his wife perished in 1945 in Auschwitz.) Even supplies to the project centers were not forthcoming—even though replacements were needed as the stockpile of materials diminished. Nevertheless, the artists found supplies and worked to the very end of the war (which meant for some the end of their lives). There are works dated as early as 1939 by Leo Haas, Nisko, Poland, and those dated as late as May 1945 by Aldo Carpi in Gusen. Sadly enough, many of the works survived their creators, some of whom perished only hours before the liberation of their respective camps.[1]

Osias Hofstatter recounts that his sister, who was living in Switzerland for a time, was able to send him supplies while he was in Gurs. As time went on and the situation worsened for all, he had to resort to his own means. "I found a little 'cahier' [a lined notepad] which I managed to get to draw on."

Alfred Kantor received packages in Auschwitz and Schwarzheide from his sister in Prague, who was not incarcerated because of her marriage to a Christian. He said: "To this day I can offer no conceivable explanation as to why the SS allowed these packages to get through." That statement typifies the Nazis' ambiguous and unpredictable temperament, with which all the inmates had to deal.

Various international relief agencies sent supplies to the Gurs Camp, including musical instruments and art materials. The artists of Gurs had adequate supplies of canvas, sketch-pads, pencils, paints, and paintbrushes during 1940 and 1941. They were able to hold two large exhibits during 1941; the first was held during the spring in one crowded barracks in the men's compound. The second exhibit, held during the summer of 1941, filled three barracks and also attracted buyers from the surrounding region. Among those artists exhibiting were Felix Nussbaum and Karl Schweisig. It

Osias Hofstatter   St. Cyprien Camp
Pencil on graph paper, 4″ × 6″
Courtesy Osias Hofstatter

is here, too, that Osias Hofstatter met Karl Schweisig, whom he felt was a master and who encouraged him, a beginner, to draw.

As helpful as it was, even this acquisition of material left the artists to fend for themselves. Halina Olomucki saved some of the paper on which she had to do her assignments to do her own work. She hid the materials as well as her work in her bunk until she could use them.

Materials—Surfaces and Media

The artists worked on any surface that would take an image. For the drawings they used tissue paper (sometimes confiscated by work details from the Nazi toilets for their artist friends), tissue for rolling cigarettes, matchbox covers, stamp sheet margins, backs of graph sheets, posters, medical report papers, wrapping paper, bags—any scrap became a possible surface for the artists. Sometimes shreds of paper were pieced together to make a surface large enough upon which to draw. As a doctor in the camp, Karel Fleischmann used the application forms for medical examinations for some of his masterful drawings. Esther Lurie was given the wrappings from the rolls of cotton that a doctor in the Leibitz infirmary saved for her. Karl Schweisig used the blank margins of postage stamp sheets for his exquisite miniatures. Alfred Kantor sought out those who worked in the administrative offices for pencil and paper in Terezin, and while in Auschwitz he was befriended by a doctor who gave him paper. Alexander Bogen found wrapping paper which he used for some of his work while he was in the forests. Bertalan Gondor used blank postcards and Franciszek Jazwiecki did portraits on paper the size of postcards. At his workbench in the armaments factory where he worked, Zoran Music tore out sheets upon which to draw from planbooks and at times from his own workbook.

When the supply of canvas ran out, the artists found old bed linen and burlap from potato sacks and the rough muslin of flour bags as substitute surfaces for their work. Petr Kien in Terezin used burlap for some of his oils.

The artists used any medium within their grasp to make their statements. The media used were pencil (writing and grease), charcoal, ink, ruddle, chalk; and pastels, watercolors, gouaches, and a few oils.

The most versatile and available of all the media was, of course, pencil. Pencil was used for administrative work, the writing of directives, keeping records, marking equipment, and for simple communication within the camp complex. It was the most commonly used material. Another pencil, referred to in some of the archives as "black chalk or pastel," resembles on close inspection the black conte crayon or the lithograph pencil which renders an intense, deep black; shading is a characteristic technique of this material.

The quivering linear drawings of Halina Olomucki, the delicate drawings of Irene Awret while in Malines Camp in Belgium, the work of Aizik Feder and Bucanek, the portrait by Peter Edel, are only some of the pencil works.

Because it could be fabricated, charcoal was also commonly used by camp artists. It is a form of carbon produced by slow burning of wood or other organic material and produces a grey-to-black image when used for drawing. This material can be blended or rubbed to get chiaroscuro effects (tonal qualities), and to achieve depth and dimension. It is remarkable that so many works in charcoal have been salvaged. Charcoal is an impermanent material, and crumbles and flakes very easily if not handled deftly or used on the appropriate surfaces. The ideal surface for charcoal is a paper with a texture or "tooth," such that the charcoal is forced into the grooves and becomes impregnated into the paper. The texture actually acts as little files that shave off the carbon and settle it into the grooves. Since the artists had very little choice in the selection of the surface, most used were not particularly good for charcoal drawings and the drawings would have been lost under normal circumstances. For some reason this did not happen. There are innumerable charcoal works that have been preserved without the use of the usual paper surfaces or precautions. Still impressively intact are the works of such artists as Bedrich Fritta, Aizik Feder, Osias Hofstatter, and Alexander Bogen.

Alexander Bogen made his own charcoal by burning dry twigs while he was in the forests. He is the only one I know who "fixed" his charcoals by using milk as the mordant or fixative.

There is an unsubstantiated account about Otto Ungar while he was confined in Buchenwald. It describes an artist with a mutilated stump of a hand drawing with a chunk of coal, wood, or something like that "on fragments of paper." As far as I know, none of these drawings has been found, but Ungar was in Buchenwald, having survived the march from Auschwitz, and the deliberate mutilation of his hand by the Nazis in Terezin left it a broken stump. He did die a few days after the liberation and perhaps with him went the secret of his Buchenwald drawings.

Halina Olomucki Auschwitz Camp (1944)
Charcoal drawing on paper fragment, 2″ × 3″
Courtesy Halina Olomucki

Alexander Bogen "En Route"
Charcoal drawing, 8″ × 10″
Courtesy Alexander Bogen

Mieczyslaw Koscielniak Ebensee Camp, 1945
Drawing, 5″ × 7¼″
Courtesy Auschwitz Memorial Museum

Records, graphs, and maps were done in pen and ink. *Tinten-stift* (copying ink) was also used to scribble the numbers on the skins of the dead corpses before they were thrown into primitive coffins in Dachau,[2] and to write numbers on the uniforms of the prisoners.

The concentration camp pen-and-ink drawings run the gamut from simple linear works to more intricate compositions. Cross-hatching is typical of pen and inks to achieve tonal qualities and dimension. Also characteristic of this medium is its use for wash drawings. This particular technique produces a watercolor effect in black and white and shades of grey. The ink is flowed onto the paper with water or blended with the ink. It, too, achieves tonal qualities and dimension, if so desired.

Esther Lurie's pen and inks, Bedrich Fritta's masterful drawings, and the works of Jo Spier are striking examples of skillful use of lines. The wash drawings of Karel Fleischmann and Otto Ungar are most accomplished statements, as are the washes of Leo Haas, which look so much like lithographs, of which he was a master. Many others used this medium. Zoran Music, for example, stretched his ink with water to increase his meagre supply.[3]

Henry Pieck, a prisoner in Wing C of Scheveningen prison in Holland, and later Buchenwald, used the black pastel or black "chalk," as did Felix Bloch and Adolf Aussenberg. In Terezin, Petr Kien used a material called "ruddle," whose chalklike appearance is reminiscent of the red-chalk drawings of the Renaissance. Ruddle is closer in color, however, to the terra cotta or sepia tones of conte crayons, and comes from red ocher, a clay colored by iron oxide and used in some parts of Europe to mark sheep.[4] In Auschwitz, Mieczyslaw Koscielniak did his drawing, "Kameradendiest," with a *braune Kreide* (brown chalk or crayon), which again resembles our sepia conte more than chalk.

Watercolors were produced in a few camps and ghettos. Halina Olomucki was given "aquarellas" in Birkenau, and Felix Nussbaum did a highly regarded watercolor (mixed media) in Gurs. Dinah Gottliebova's Auschwitz portraits of gypsies were done in watercolor. Those supplies which the SS provided for their work permitted the artists to "borrow" what they could for their secret works.

Otto Ungar did many works in gouache. Worked much like oils, gouache is ordinarily used on heavy paper or cardboard. A watercolor, unusual for historical value, was done by an artist named "Schloll" in June of 1941, who was imprisoned in Ferra-

Charlotte Buresova "Deportation," Terezin Camp (1942)
Oil on canvas, 12" × 15"
Courtesy Biet Lohamel Haghetaot

monti Camp in Italy. It shows the room of the *capo* of the barracks. On the reverse side is the vitae of the *capo* Dr. Maximillian Perelez, who was apparently highly respected by his fellow inmates. This drawing-citation was a gift from the prisoners to Dr. Perelez. To date, there is no other information about "Schloll."[5]

There were a few pastels done by interned artists. This material has characteristics of charcoal but also has color. A number of portraits in pastels were done by Aizik Feder in Drancy. He also combined other media, such as pencil and charcoal, in his works. Even fewer oils have been recovered and it is probable that few were done. Nonetheless, Charlotte Buresova's tiny oils have been salvaged and are in the collection of the Biet Lohamei Haghetaot in Asherat, Israel. The largest collection of oils, painted by Petr Kien, is in Terezin Memorial Museum.

Artists such as Aizik Feder and Felix Nussbaum combined media. This makes it difficult to fit them into any category. The categorization made here is solely to show the artists' versatility and ingenuity, and the extent to which they went to work.

Works that are hard to categorize are montages of Simon Wiesenthal, which he did in Mauthausen, and Frantisek Zelenka's scenery designs for the performances in Terezin of Gogol's *Wedding*. Exquisite are Zelenka's costume designs for such Czech plays as Gerron's *Karussell*, the Czech folk play, *Esther and the King*, and the costume for the dancer in Karel Svenk's *The Last Cyclist*. Into what slot would fit the marionette theater and cardboard puppets that Leon Landau made for the children of Malines Camp? Where would one put the diaries of Liesel Felsenthal, Charlotte Salomon, and Jan Budding, or the miniatures of Karl Schweisig?

Tools

As ingenious as *finding* materials was the *improvising* of tools. Initially, Esther Lurie had no pens in Leibitz so she used chips of wood, dipping them in ink in order to draw the women slave laborers. These drawings have been saved and are in the collection of the Beit Lohamei Haghetoat in Israel, and are also compiled in a moving book, *Jewesses in Slavery*. Alexander Bogen not only made his own charcoal and devised a way to use milk, when he could get it, as a fixative, he also did woodcuts using wood he found in the forest and his penknife as a chisel. The partisans had a small mobile press for circulars they distributed in the ghetto which he used to print his woodcuts.

Esther Lurie Leibitz Camp (1944)
Ink drawing done with wood chips, 3 ″ × 5 ″
Courtesy Esther Lurie

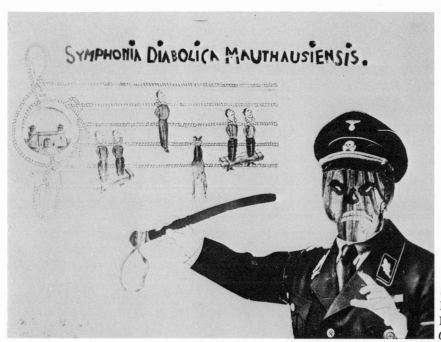

SYMPHONIA DIABOLICA MAUTHAUSIENSIS.

Simon Wiesenthal
Mauthausen Camp (1945)
Montage
Courtesy Simon Wiesenthal

When the artists had no brushes for their wash drawings or watercolors, they devised ways to paint by making strips or chips from cardboard or cloth or any material that would help flow the image onto the paper. Often they would use their fingers. One small watercolor of an interior of a barrack room done with fingers as tools is in the collection at the Museum in Asherat.

Other Data

The works range in size from small to minuscule; the average size is around 8" × 10". A few pieces are unusually large when one considers the circumstances under which they were produced. For example, some of the works by Fritta in the Prague State Jewish Museum measure about 20" × 30" — rather large for a work that had to be hidden. Another artist who did some fairly large pieces (relative to others done in the camps) is Karel Fleischmann. Some of his works are as large as Fritta's. The works of Leo Haas and Otto Ungar are in this size range as well.

Many works cannot be measured because they were done on scraps that make measurement impossible. Halina Olomucki's drawing done on tissue, for example, or the tiny pencil drawing she did on a scrap of paper were mere fragments. Esther Lurie hid her drawings in her clothing for eight months and thus, they are crumpled and small. There are pieces by the artists in the collection at Yad Vashem Memorial Museum which measure as small as 2" × 5". The diary of Liesel Felsenthal — the teen-ager from Mannheim, Germany imprisoned in Gurs — is 2" × 3", and Karl Schweisig's postage-stamp-size drawings, the tiniest in existence, are 1" × ¾". There are accounts that some drawings were done on matchbox covers and the drawings Alfred Kantor did in Schwarzheide measure 3" × 4".

The majority of works that have been recovered are drawings. In this medium, improvisation was more possible, statements could be made more rapidly (no drying time, as demanded by other media, was required), the works could be done on smaller and more varied surfaces, and could be more easily concealed.

Drawings done in the camps were not intended as sketches or cartoons to be explored or completed later in another medium, nor were they adjuncts of any other technique. Unwittingly, the artists of the camps revived the importance of drawing as an art form, and they stretched its characteristics and its potentials to the limits.

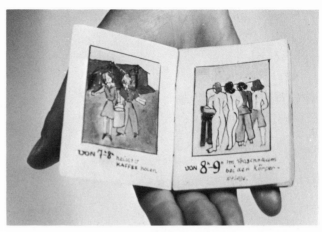

Liesel Felsenthal (Basnitzki)
"Diary" (two pages), Camp de Gurs (1941)
Watercolor, 2″ × 3″
Courtesy Liesel Felsenthal (Basnitzki)

Karl Schweisig Camp de Gurs (1941)
Colored ink drawings on blank margin
of stamp sheets, 1″ × ¾″
Courtesy Leo Baeck Institute, New York

Josef Richter Sobibor Camp (1943)
Pencil drawing on newsprint fragment, 3″ × 4½″
Courtesy Biet Lohamel Haghetaot

Bruno Apitz "The Last Expression,"
Buchenwald Camp (1944–1945)
Wood carving, 12″ × 8″ × 3″
Courtesy Buchenwald Memorial Museum

Anton Suchecki "Prisoner in Wood,"
Auschwitz Camp (1940–1942)
Wood carving, 4″ high
Courtesy Auschwitz Memorial Museum

In the hands of an artist any material available may become a tool for expressing a thought. Lack of materials or ideal situations are obviously not deterrents to creativity, nor is improvisation new to artists. Elaborate equipment or facilities are not as important after all as knowing the craft well enough that clever substitutions can be made through inventiveness. The artists in the camps proved this. For example, how did Alexander Bogen know that milk could be used as a mordant? How could the artists make charcoal? History has proven that those artists who have had an inherent sensitivity and skill for interpretation, but also knew the pragmatics, the chemistry of these materials, have done the works that have lasted through centuries.[6] The artists in the camps made what seems impossible possible with the most menial materials of the poorest quality through their unquestionable ability to improvise.

While drawings were the most prevalent form discovered, even sculpture was done in the camps. Difficult to conceal because of its bulk, some sculpture was done on assignment, and some secretly.

In the carpenters' workshop in Auschwitz, sculptures were carved out of wood. One example of the work done there is a small figure of a prisoner called *Haftlingsfigur Aus Holz* ("prisoner in wood") by Anton Suchecki, circa 1942. According to the Auschwitz Museum curator, there are a number of sculptures in that collection and another account claims that there are close to a hundred pieces there.[7]

A number of artists did sculpture in Terezin. The prolific Bedrich Fritta modeled a high relief panel, which has been salvaged, of a prisoners transport. Incarcerated a short time in Terezin, Arnold Zadikow, a sculptor whose life work was almost entirely destroyed by the Nazis as decadent art, apparently did sculpture there too, although little of this Czech sculptor's work is known to have been salvaged. Among the works of Rudolf Saudek are a small figure, a head, a small sculpture of Eve, and a *bas-relief*.[8] There is a small terra-cotta head about four inches high at the Terezin Memorial, modeled by Professor Karel Stipl who was a member of the Fine Arts Academy in Prague. When he was imprisoned in Terezin, friends outside the camp sneaked clay in to him and other prisoners stood watch as he worked. Casts were made of the head after the war. Only two of these cast pieces are known to be in existence. The original has been lost.

While imprisoned in Terezin, Alois Bucanek was assigned to work with the doctors in the sick ward where prisoners with typhus

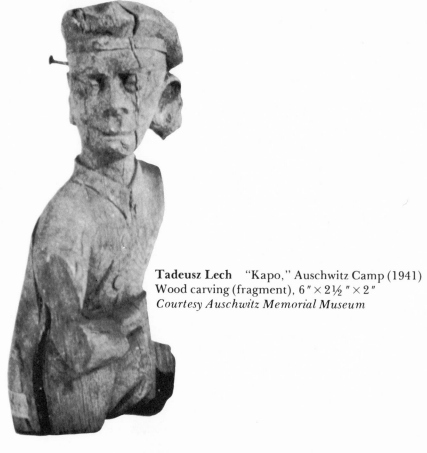

Tadeusz Lech   "Kapo," Auschwitz Camp (1941)
Wood carving (fragment), 6″ × 2½″ × 2″
Courtesy Auschwitz Memorial Museum

Albin Boniecki   "Tortoise," Maidanek Camp (1941–1944)
Cement sculpture, 3′ × 2′ × 1½′
Courtesy Buchenwald Memorial Museum

were confined. He was permitted to use the sick prisoners as models not only for his drawings but for his sculptures as well. While he was doing portrait studies of some of the prisoners they succumbed to the deadly typhus. Believing that Bucanek was responsible for their deaths, panic broke out in the sick room every time the sculptor appeared. The prisoners believed that they would die if he modeled them so he had to stop. Soon after, Bucanek himself contracted typhus, and died in the small fortress in Terezin on September 9, 1945.[9]

Messages for resistance were conveyed in many ways and there are many samples of the methods used to communicate by the resistance groups. At times these messages were openly expressed in symbols understood only by the prisoners. The symbol of the tortoise, for example, was synonymous with the resistance. It meant a deliberate slow down in operations of any work or assignment that the Nazis enforced on the prisoners for the war. Members of the resistance painted the sign of the tortoise on buildings to remind the prisoners and to encourage them.[10] In the Maidanek death camp, a group of prisoners got SS consent to do some sculpture. A sculpture in cement, done sometime between 1941 and 1944 by Albin Bonieki, was of a tortoise. So the artists using a secret symbol openly defied their captors who had unwittingly assented to the creation of the work.

Although artists have indeed improvised under all sorts of conditions, at no place and at no time in history was a group faced with problems and challenges as enormous as those confronting the artists of the concentration and death camps. The prolific output, the foresight to hide their works, is awesome. We are left with these talismans, the thousands of fragments forever forged and stamped into the history of the twentieth century. Primo Levi, the Italian-Jewish author confined in Auschwitz wrote: "even in this place one must want to survive, to tell the story, to bear witness."[11]

Halina Olomucki
Warsaw Ghetto (1943)
Charcoal on tissue paper,
6½ ″ × 9¾ ″
Courtesy M. Novitch

My friends in the Block knew that I drew. They said to me, "It is terrible here, so draw always, paint always, and remember always. Remember us always. At least through your drawings we will live." I promised them I would do this. Each time I recall those days, and each time I have an exhibit, I always include a work commemorating them. I cannot forget, I cannot forget! They always live with me and I think often about those days.

Halina Olomucki
Artist-survivor
Holon, Israel, 1979

7

Search Everywhere in Every Inch of Soil:

The Hidden and the Recovered Works

A notebook written in Yiddish was found in Auschwitz, stuffed into an aluminum German canteen with a metal stopper. In it Sonderkommando Salmen Gradowski wrote:

> Dear finder, search everywhere in every inch of soil. Tens of documents are buried under it, mine and those of other persons, which will throw light on everything that was happening here. Great quantities of teeth are buried here. It was we, the Kommando workers, who expressly have strewn them all over the terrain, as many as we could so that the world should find material traces of the millions of the murdered.

Gradowski perished in the revolt in Auschwitz. His manuscript was found in the course of the excavations in the site of Crematorium II at Birkenau on March 5, 1945.[1]

The marvel swells from the "found objects" which the artists managed to scrape up for their works to the hiding places, and the methods devised for the preservation of their art. The artists' works were hidden in the barrack walls, buried in the ground, concealed in bunks and lofts of buildings, tucked into their tattered clothing, or smuggled out of the camps. Always under scrutiny, they took great pains to find the ways and means to protect their works. Whenever possible they passed them on by hand via prisoners leaving on transports or going to work in crews into the nearby village,

135

or by bribing the guards. All were dangerous ventures and involved much planning, forethought, and sheer nerve.

The artists searched for ready-made containers or constructed them themselves. Glass jars, cardboard boxes, ceramic urns, milk cans, heavy paper or oil-cloth wrappers, rolls from toilet tissue, anything that would act as a covering, became possible containers in which to conceal their works. This was an arduous task that posed many problems. By their very nature artworks were harder to conceal than the smaller written messages that were ingeniously sent out by active resistance groups like the one at Auschwitz. Coded messages were written on thin paper used for rolling cigarettes and inserted into hollowed-out candles, empty fountain pens, cigarettes, keys, and other innocent-looking objects that would not arouse suspicion. Most of these messages were written in Block 10, the camp hospital, in a room bearing an official notice, *Fleckfieberverdacht* ("typhus suspected") which kept the ever-threatening SS away out of fear of contagion.[2]

Hiding Places

On a balmy summer afternoon in her studio-apartment in Tel Aviv, Esther Lurie related what she did about her work:

> I thought of asking the Jewish potters in the ghetto to pre-pare several large jars [urns] for me in order to hide my pic-tures in them. I had at least two hundred watercolors and drawings by this time, although I had given a few to Mr. Tory to keep with his archives. They were about 35 cm by 25 cm. The potters were willing to help me. How I would hide them when the moment came gave me no rest. On the day of the *Aktion*, October 26, 1943, when three thousand Jews from the ghetto were taken away, I placed my pictures in the jars, and buried them in the ground in the cellar of my sister's house. I dug the hole myself. By this time the ghetto had its status changed to Konzentrationslager Kauen. We were now a camp. By 1944 the camp was liqui-dated and they sent me with the other women to Stutthof Concentration Camp. I had to leave my work behind where I had buried it. I believe they are still there and I want to go back to get them. I wanted to draw all this but it was dan-gerous and difficult, now. A girl working at the registering of prisoners gave me some poor quality paper. On these sheets I did drawings which I hid in my clothes where they remained for the months we spent in the labor camp. They are rubbed and creased and wrinkled and do not lend them-selves to reproduction.[3]

"We hid our works in several ways," Leo Haas explained to me:

I had a friend who was an architect, and we found a box which we lined with tin he had found. How he found the tin, I don't know, but we used it. In the box Fritta and I put our drawings. Then with feverish efforts we pried out a part of the wall of our room, we placed the box in it and then bricked up the wall. We carefully replaced the bricks and dirtied up the mortar so that no one could tell that the wall had been tampered with. Some of the works we buried in the ground outside the barracks.

Otto Ungar hid his drawings in the loft of his building in Terezin. He buried the largest body of his works in the barrack courtyard. Moritz Nagel hid his drawings in the attic of one of the houses in the Terezin Ghetto.

Bunks were the hiding places for Halina Olomucki and Ella Lieberman Shiber. Other drawings the size of postcards were found under the rotten straw on a bunk in Auschwitz. Jozef Szajna's friends brought him paper and pencil while he was confined in the *Krankenhaus* (the camp hospital) in Birkenau. Twenty of these drawings he hid under the straw mattress of his hospital cot.[4]

Zoran Music hid his drawings in the munitions plant where he worked in Dachau. When the plant was bombed he found only thirty-five of over one hundred eighty pieces that he had done.

Aldo Carpi's diary was finally hidden under the wooden floor of the infirmary in Gusen. He wrote:

I didn't know what to do. I got a black envelope and I slipped in it some of my pages and placed it in the inner pocket of my jacket. I hid some in a pair of old trousers and thrust them into the foot of an old urn in the pathology room. The risks we were running, my papers and I, augmented our misery. It seemed all that was good is in these papers.

Alexander Bogen buried his drawings in the ground of the Narocz Forest.

I had a lot of drawings. What can I do with them? We had to escape because the Germans were approaching. I found a glass or something like that and hurriedly buried them in the ground. In the autumn of 1943 when Vilna was being destroyed, I was helping a group of Jews to escape into the forest. One of the girls fell, and as I pulled her to safety for the Germans were almost upon us, my sketchbook fell to the ground and its sheets scattered all over. I tried to collect

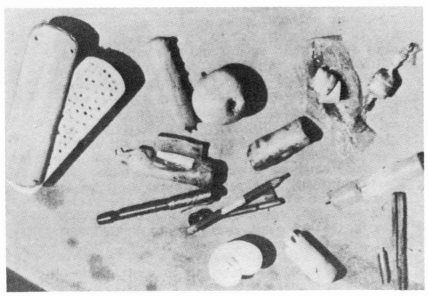

Objects used by the Resistance to conceal messages
Courtesy Auschwitz Memorial Museum

Jozef Szajna   "Block 11," Auschwitz Camp (1943)
Pencil, 8″ × 10″
Courtesy Auschwitz Memorial Museum

them but there was a howling wind, and instead they were blown in every direction. I managed to grab a few and ran into the forest with my companions. This was my *Diary of an Artist*! Nothing is left of it except the few scraps which are in my book.

Avraham Golub-Tory hid some of Esther Lurie's works along with the archives of the Kovno Ghetto under the concrete foundations of a three-story building in Block Z of that ghetto. At the end of the war he retrieved all the documents. A tireless searcher of evidence in the form of the arts, Miriam Novitch, tells me that she helped hide the works of the poet, Yitzhak Katzenelson. The poetry written on tissue paper was rolled into the cardboard rolls of toilet tissue, and buried. Years later, she returned to find them intact.[5]

Sometimes friends of the artists dared to smuggle out drawings. Alfred Kantor relates:

The few Schwarzheide drawings that actually survive did so through the bravery of a friend who smuggled them out [in Terezin]. . . . I acquired a note book which I filled with sketches. . . . when I was ordered to leave Terezin for Auschwitz in 1943, I entrusted my notebook to a friend who stayed in Terezin, and returned it to me after I was liberated. Most of my sketches I had to destroy to avoid being caught [in Schwarzheide] but once drawn these sketches could never be erased from my mind. I committed them to memory and as soon as I was free again drawing came rapidly to me and the rescued material made it possible for me to put together my diary.[6]

After his murder, trusted and courageous friends of poet-artist Josef Capek kept the works that he had done in Buchenwald and Sachsenhausen safely until their liberation. Preserved are several groups of small drawings and two paintings, now located in the Terezin Memorial Museum.

The large body of works by Karel Fleischmann was saved by the resistance group in Terezin. After the war Dr. Fleischmann's brother gave the entire collection to the Prague State Jewish Museum.

Artists' works were smuggled out of Auschwitz by way of the *Waschetransport* ("laundry wagons") of the SS. Before the laundry was taken to the nearby town, the prisoners would put their messages and drawings in between the clothing. The bribed guards would then take them to the outside.[7]

In Auschwitz many drawings were also sent out of the camp by the *Haftlingspost—von hand zu hand* ("prisoners' mail—from hand to hand"). This is what the prisoners called their method of passing their works onto the labor crews who worked outside the camp. They would entrust their works to these workers, who would "drop them off" en route.[8]

Those who managed to escape would take messages and art work. One such prisoner of about the 150 who escaped safely from Auschwitz was Wincenty Gawron, who took with him caricatures of the SS and the *capos* that he had drawn, and many drawings of other artists, such as Stanislaw Gutkiewicz and Leo Turalski. After the war he presented these works to the Auschwitz Memorial Museum.[9]

Alexander Bogen described how some of his works were saved:

When we knew that Vilna was going to be destroyed we [partisans] tried to rescue the people. One of those I saved was my friend, the famous poet Abraham Sutzkever. We went into the forest where the Russian troops had joined us and were taking our wounded by plane to Moscow. Because he was the important and well-known poet, Sutzkever was taken to Moscow, too. As we were parting, I asked, "Abraham, please take my drawings with you." He did and they were exhibited in Moscow.

It is equally amazing that some artists, when concealing their work, left "wills" directing where their work should be sent by any finder. In his opening address at the trial of Eichmann in Israel, the eloquent Gideon Hausner states that "many last messages bequeathed by the dead were scribbled on scraps of paper, hidden in the sewing machines of the Chelmno Death Camp, and scratched with fingernails on the walls of gas chambers in Maidanek."[10] Drawings were also scratched and drawn on the cell walls and barrack ceilings in some of the prisons where the artists were held (the walls at Fort Breendonk,[11] Auschwitz, and the ceiling at Birkenau B 1b). Esther Lurie left a will and testament: "anyone who might find these drawings at some future time, [I request] to forward them to the Tel Aviv Museum."[12]

Some left very specific instructions about what was to be done with their material if and when found. An unknown author whose manuscript was disinterred in the summer of 1952 at the site of Crematorium 111 in Birkenau expressed a wish that all his discovered works should be published under the title, *Amidst a Night-*

mare of Crime. He also designated that more notes "are to be found in the various boxes and jars on the terrain of the yard, Crematorium 111 and under the mound of bones on the site of Crematorium 11.[13]

The artist, Gela Seksztein, who perished in the Treblinka gas chambers, left this message with her art works, which were found along with the archives of the Warsaw Ghetto: "August 1, 1942, Warsaw, I have been condemned to death. I must die and I have done everything I had to do, first hide my works. Adieu, Jewish People! Don't allow such a catastrophe to happen again."[14]

Many other documents have been disinterred. Messages from the underground and the resistance movements in the camps have been uncovered: the diaries of Chaim Kaplan, and of Emmanuel Ringelblum, whose archive was found in two sections under the ruin and rubble of the Warsaw Ghetto.[15] The diary of Anne Frank was found after the war on the floor where it had dropped when she and her family were captured. There were artists who left pictorial diaries: Charlotte Salomon, the young Liesel Felsenthal in Gurs, and Jan Budding, who was incarcerated in Sachsenhausen. He left a series of drawings done on rough scraps of paper, and a diary with tiny illustrations in the margins about his experiences in Sachsenhausen. Aldo Carpi's diary, hand written with accompanying drawings in Gusen, is in two volumes. One is bound in cardboard and the striped cloth of the prisoner's uniform, the other with an X-ray sheet. Both are in the Vatican collection.

Recovery

After the liberation, those who survived made every effort to return to where their works and works of their friends had been hidden. Some succeeded, some were unable or not permitted to go back to certain places, some could not find the work. Many of the artists perished and with them their secret hiding places. Many artists working independently do not know the whereabouts of their works, some of which were destroyed by bombings, and all kinds of predators, or left in the haste of escape or rescue.

Of the two hundred drawings and paintings that Esther Lurie did in Kovno, only eleven were found. Those that were buried under the cellar of her sister's home have not been uncovered as far as Esther Lurie knows. Those that were buried with the records and other works of young Nolick under Block Z, Avraham Tory returned to Esther when they met after the war. As certain as Esther Lurie is that her works are still where she left them, is Mr. Tory that they were destroyed. He told me:

> I returned to Block Z to retrieve that part of Esther's work and the other records that I had kept in trust. They were all there where I had left them. When I went to Esther's sister's house, I found the building had fallen prey to war. . . . It no longer existed. . . . I searched through the rubble but could find none of the art she had hidden there.

Esther Lurie, however, believes they are there and only she knows where to find them.

After the liberation from Mauthausen, Leo Haas went back to Terezin to find his wife who had been in the Kleine Festung all this time, a partial invalid as a result of the brutal treatment there. In spite of this she had managed to care for Bedrich Fritta's son Tommy, who had been orphaned, and whom the Haases adopted. Returning to the "hiding places," he found intact all the work that he and Fritta had hidden: "I sought out the places where our works had been placed and they were all there. Fritta's wonderful cycle of 150 drawings, all my work, they were all there and I was surprised to see, in good condition."

Halina Olomucki returned to Auschwitz-Birkenau and found about twenty of her drawings still under the straw in her bunk.

Alexander Bogen returned to Narocz Lake to find his works:

> I searched everywhere but I could not find the place where I put them. It was very difficult to find them in that vast forest. The hasty escape from the Germans did not permit a marker, and the enormous Lake of Narocz is bordered by the vast forest that spans from Vilna to Smolensk in White Russia.

The works of Otto Ungar that were hidden in the loft were probably taken by the prisoners and friends as they were liberated. The large collection in the courtyard was unearthed in January of 1946. Dr. George Maleninsky and Yaroslava Bezdekova, the chief archivist at the Terezin Museum, claim that the major part of this collection is in the possession of the Ungar family in Brno.[16]

In October of 1950, in an attic of one of the buildings in Terezin Ghetto, some two hundred gouaches, watercolors, and drawings by Moritz Nagel were found where he had hidden them. Nagel worked in the "Technical Department" in Terezin. In his free time

Moritz Nagel　Terezin Camp
Watercolor, 8″ × 10″
Courtesy Yad Vashem Memorial Museum

he drew for friends and worked on a collection for himself. Nagel perished in Auschwitz in 1944.[17]

When the American troops liberated the camps, many prisoners gave whatever they had to show their gratitude to their liberators. Some of these were drawings given either by artists or friends who had the drawings. Dr. Marcus Smith, a medical officer in the American liberation forces, recounts not only his experiences in his fine and informative book, *Dachau: The Harrowing of Hell*, but includes as illustrations the works that a prisoner gave him when his medical unit was being moved.[18] Another medic, Dr. Edwin Smolin, also was given a drawing.[19] These happen to be by Zoran Music of Venice who was confined in Dachau. In our conversation Zoran Music remembers "having given some drawings to an American official at the moment of liberation."

When the Russian troops liberated Auschwitz, a prisoner gave some of Dinah Gottliebova's portraits to a young Polish boy who had come to the camp looking for someone. Later the boy's family gave these drawings to the Auschwitz Memorial Museum.

The bereaved parents of Peter Ginz gave their dead son's writings and art works to Yad Vashem Memorial Museum in Israel and some remained in the Terezin Memorial Museum. The drawings of Norbert Troller, the architect in Terezin who did many drawings of children, were found intact after the liberation. Alfred Kantor recalls that his drawings were made at the urging of

> coprisoners for a little booklet of our activities to be presented to the camp leader on his birthday. When we learned that said camp leader was a two-faced creature, his second (ugly) face, heretofore hidden from us came to the surface at some occasion—the project was cancelled and the prisoner who had commissioned me to do the artwork—simply kept it for himself. (Succeeded in rescuing it when on the death march.)[20]

As searchers found the messages and as excavations during and after liberation were conducted and unearthed even more documents, news of these discoveries spread. This news brought to the camp sites many who hoped to find some clue or trace of family or relatives among the ashes and rubble. Attracted to these sites were also collectors, such as Miriam Novitch, the art curator of the Biet Lohamei Haghetoat. In an article she wrote for an Italian publication and sent to me, she explains:

I am a member of a small group that survives. Now there are only ten of us and we live in a kibbutz in Israel called the *Biet Lohamei Haghetaot*, (Ghetto Fighters House). For thirty years we have dedicated ourselves to the search for documents—proof to all—of what befell our people. We go searching for them in every corner of the globe.[21]

In some cases government officials interceded for the artists who were unable to get the works that they knew had been recovered. Alexander Bogen tells:

In 1959 when I left Poland to come to Israel, I was stopped at the border and my work, that I had saved because it stayed with me, some 60 or 70 pieces, were taken from me at the border. They [the officials] claimed that they belonged to the Polish culture and had to stay there and were eventually put on exhibit at the museum in Warsaw. I came to Israel without one of my drawings. Some time later, with the intercession of the president of Israel, at that time Ben Zvi, who was involved with the research of documents done during this time and with [by] diplomatic means my work was returned to me. The Polish Embassy which was in Israel at that time called me one day and said they had a package for me. It was a box of my drawings.

One of Esther Lurie's drawings of the city of Kovno was found in the office of a German officer. After the war it was sent to the museum in Vilna. After inquiries by the Israeli foreign ministers and by the intercession of Golda Meir herself, who was at that time the ambassador to Moscow, the drawing was given to Mrs. Meir, who recognized it as Esther Lurie's. She returned it to the artist and it is today in a private collection in the United States.

It can be said that there were almost as many ways to conceal and methods to preserve the works as there were artists in the camps. All who engaged in secret work were inordinately determined in the solution of their unique problems, all identical in their motivation. Many works and documents, records and messages were recovered after liberation as excavations at the sites continued for various reasons. Some were not found until by accident years later and there is no way to gauge how many were destroyed along with the masses of people. Many believe, like Esther Lurie, that works are still buried and must be retrieved. On October 17, 1962, a jar was found buried near Crematorium 111 in Birkenau. A roll of papers was wrapped in oil cloth. This was the manuscript of Salmen Lewenthal. Altogether, there were seventy-five leaves of paper written on one side in the jar. Written entirely in Polish, the works deal mainly with two events in the camp: *Di 3,000 kadete* ("3,000 naked people"), and *Di 600 inglekh* ("600 boys").[22]

It is difficult to estimate how much work was done or how much has been salvaged. There are people who own works who are unaware of their importance. It is true that thousands of pieces have been miraculously recovered, and are in archives, museums, and documentation centers throughout the United States, Europe, Israel, and the USSR. It appears also to be true that most of the art works that have been found were those done in secret, possibly because the assigned or "official" work was destroyed along with other records.

When the Nazis were preparing the camps for evacuation and demolition because of the advancing Allied forces, hundreds of records and documents, buildings—entire camp sites—were set on fire or blown up. Just as the wave of Nazi terrorism years before set to the torch the books and great works of art, and murdered more than twelve million people in their rampage across the continent of Europe, so again in retreat they foraged a trail of the destruction of every vestige of the promise that the thousand-year Reich had in store for humankind. They succeeded neither in conquest nor in concealment of the truth, and this is perhaps the caveat to those of this breed. The evidence of what this society nurtured keeps cropping up like perennial foliage. In Auschwitz-Birkenau

> somewhere among the ruins there lay a tin bowl from which some prisoner had probably eaten his watery soup. He had awkwardly scratched on it a boat floating at the mercy of a raging sea. Above there was an inscription, "don't forget the forlorn man." On the back of the bowl an airplane was seen with the American star on its wings in the act of letting a bomb fall. The inscription above that picture was, "VOX DEI" [voice of God].[23]

How many more art works and materials are still to be unearthed? What is concealed under that gentle-looking mantle of green that covers so many memorial grounds? What lies under the tranquil-looking fields that shield the shame in the land of camps? What do the forests deep in the darkness of their overgrowths enshroud? A land fraught with so much hallowed ground must cradle more secrets in its blood-soaked bosom.

A child-man-author bequeathed:

It's up to you, Your task is to rid the world of the war storm, to build a barrier. You must place yourselves under your banner—the best one . . . and do not let your banner be a mere rag: the banner must be your shield, the shield of justice, truth, and love. —Hanus Pollak, *Vedem* ("We're Leading") (part of a manuscript found on July 4, 1950, in Terezin).

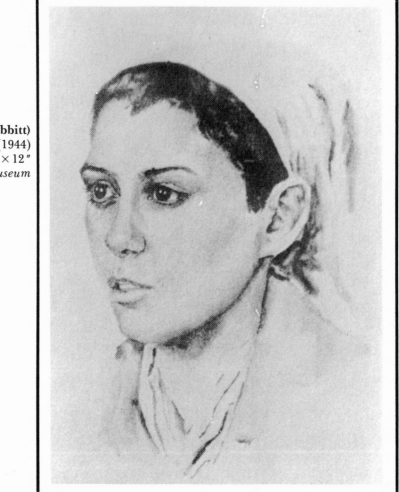

Dinah Gottliebova (Babbitt)
"French Gypsy," Auschwitz Camp (1944)
Watercolor, 15"×12"
Courtesy Auschwitz Memorial Museum

I don't think my story will be of any use to you, but reading
about all the noble artists trying to let the world know—puts me
in awe and I wish, I could now in retrospect do something. Time
is running out however, I am fifty-seven and still earning a living pushing a pencil as assistant animator, doing Cap'n Crunch
instead of documentaries. Well—that's life—thank God!

Dinah Gottliebova-Babbitt
Santa Cruz, California
January 30, 1980

8

fragments:
The Diaspora of the Works

As unorthodox as the outburst of message art from the camps and ghettos is, equally unorthodox is the dispersal of the works. Unlike any before it, this is the diaspora of the Jews in visual imagery— messages intended to be far-reaching by the artists who created them and exceeding their hopes and dreams. Works today are in the Americas, Europe, Russia, Israel, and Australia. The dispersal is vast, as if an airplane took wing with a special cargo of messages and dropped them to scatter on the earth, and they nestled in every corner of it making the message ubiquitous. The diaspora of the Jews continues in another most unexpected idiom and unwittingly many had a part in it. By accident or by design, there are a number of factors responsible for this diaspora: records found at the sites or in abandoned buildings during excavations or "clean-up" operations, the barter system in the camps, the searches at the sites by relatives, friends, or collectors, the smuggling of works out of the camps and ghettos, and the distribution of works by individuals or organizations who offered assistance to the destitute artists after the war with promises of sales and exhibitions in other countries. This last very often resulted in the exploitation of the artists.

After the war and the liberation some of the surviving Jews tried to return to their homes only to find the sentiment and hostility toward them unchanged. Many could not remain. (In fact, in Kielce, Poland, in 1946, the townspeople accused the two hundred

149

Jews, remnants of the prewar Jewish population of 25,000, of ritual murder. Another pogrom killed forty-seven of the remaining Jewish populace and wounded fifty others.)[1] For moral, personal, or physical reasons many could not return to their native lands. For most there were no longer any ties in those lands, many of their homes had been decimated or expropriated by the governments or former neighbors, and in many places they were unwelcome. After the debacle, as the Jews found their way to new homes, new lands, and new lives many of them carried the artists' messages. Some were aware of the precious load and some were not.

In liberating the camps, the armed forces of both the Allies and the Russians retrieved the records and documents that had not been destroyed, and sent them to their respective countries to become part of the war records arsenals. Among the papers were drawings and other nonmilitary data.[2] The value of all documents was well known and every effort was made to preserve them. Avraham Tory, concerned when he was approached by the KGB about the Kovno Ghetto archives, and uncertain about the propriety of giving them up, sought the advice of the poet Abraham Sutzkever, who was now placed by the Russians in a position of authority in Vilna. The answer from the poet was, "Don't give them up." The records and the drawings are in Israel today.[3] Out of gratitude, some of the artist-prisoners themselves gave their drawings to the soldiers when the camps were liberated, as did other prisoners who had works in their possession.[4] In the clean-up operations the soldiers found many items, among them sketches, which were turned over to the authorities or kept as souvenirs.

Some of the families of the artists donated the art works to various museums or archives. The brother of Karel Fleischmann gave his works to the Prague State Jewish Museum,[5] and the brother of Bertalan Gondor contributed the eight pencil-drawn postcards to the Leo Baeck Archives in New York City.[6] Dinah Gottliebova-Babbitt's gypsy portraits were given by a Polish family to the Auschwitz Memorial Museum, and the works that Alfred Kantor did in Schwarzheide are privately owned in the United States by the man who smuggled them out of the camp.

Instrumental in this diaspora were the surviving artists themselves. Upon their release some of them were able to go back to the camps where they retrieved the hidden works and many gave them to museums already existing in their countries, or later to museums that were erected in commemoration of the Holocaust. Most of the artists' works from Terezin are in the Prague State Jewish Museum or the Terezin Memorial Museum because of artists like Leo Haas who gave these museums the bulk of his works and those of his friend, Fritta. Many of the artists who emigrated to Israel gave their works to museums there. An artist who escaped from Auschwitz and now lives in America later gave his drawings and those of his friends to the Auschwitz Memorial Museum.

Identification

Another interesting note is that so many of the artists signed and dated their works and at times included the name of the camp as well as the title on the front of their drawings. In fact, practically all the papers I have seen are signed and dated and many of the signatures are as individualistic as the works. More often, works are identified but the history of the artist is obscure or unknown thus far: Milada Marisova, Jurek Fuks, Mabull, and Schloll, among others. Realistic portraits carefully signed and dated were done in the Caserne Dossin in Brussels. The strong signature of Leo Haas appears on all his completed works, as does the name of the camps—among them the pencil portraits done in Nisko which also bear the title, and those in Terezin, Ebensee, Mauthausen, and Sachsenhausen. Other artists clearly inscribed and identified their works; Adolf Aussenberg, Otto Ungar, Esther Lurie, Karel Fleischmann, Petr Kien, Henry Pieck, Peter Edel, Wincenty Gawron, Zoran Music, Aldo Carpi, Aizik Feder, and so many others clearly signed their names and often included the dates, the camp names, and sometimes titles. Halina Olomucki signed only her first name and the date. These occasionally appear along the side of her drawings. A few artists signed only their last names, as did (Francisek) Jaswiecki who also included *Ozwiecim*. Some signed only their initials—among them Felix Bloch of the *Zeichenstube* Group in Terezin, who used his well-known initials, "FEB," and Alois Bucanek who used a decorative script letter, "B," both with the camp name and dates included. Some works are signed on the front with explanations on the backs. A very innocent-looking pencil drawing by Adolf Aussenberg of the Terezin ghetto town has a statement written in German on the back which says in essence, "don't judge a book by its cover."[7] The pencil-drawn postcards of Bertalan Gondor, on the other hand, passed through the mails escaping the scrutiny of the censors perhaps because of the "I-am-well-all-is-fine" message as prescribed by the Nazis although the drawings belie the message. Another artist, Henry Behr, wrote lengthy explanations

Adolf Aussenberg   Terezin Camp (1944)
Pen and ink drawing, 8″ × 10″
Courtesy Prague State Jewish Museum

Alois Bucanek   Terezin Camp (1941–1943)
Pencil drawing, 5″ × 7″
Courtesy Terezin Memorial Museum

on the back of the watercolors he did in Terezin. On the front signed and dated, the reverse side of one reads: "Most of the people died from malnutrition and weakness and others perished in the so-called death transports. One can only buy mustard for the currency issued in Therienstadt"; and on a watercolor whose title, "Terezin, Quarters L 306, 1944," appears clearly at the bottom of the work, he wrote on the back: "These quarters housed approximately 90 men who were killed. I drew this picture from my bed; the bedding and furnishings were installed only later when the propaganda film, 'The Fuhrer Gives the Jews a City,' was made. In the right foreground is a single bed which belonged to the senior prisoner in the room. He pretended to be wounded in the war but he wasn't. He also landed in a death camp where he was gassed."[8]

When I commented to Leo Haas that this was probably how the Nazis traced works to the artists in Terezin who were punished for doing *Greuelpropaganda* ("horror-propaganda art"), he disagreed: "The works found by the SS were merely sketches or unfinished pieces and therefore unsigned. When Eichmann interrogated us we each identified our own pieces. Only our finished works were signed."

Many of the works are signed and dated but there are other identifying factors. The artists were registered in the camps, as were all prisoners. Many had friends who knew about their secret work. Many worked with the underground or resistance groups and some cooperated with the archivists to keep records. The work of Karel Fleischmann was kept until the liberation by the resistance group in Terezin, and the works of Josef Capek were hidden by friends after he was sent to the death camp. Gela Seks7stein's works were found with the archives in the Warsaw Ghetto, and the works of Esther Lurie and Nolick were kept with the records in the Kovno Ghetto.

Research so far shows that seldom are the works unsigned and seldom can they not be traced to a camp or ghetto. Unsigned and unidentifiable papers are really in the minority. Some of these unsigned works were claimed after the liberation by artists who retrieved them themselves or who recognized them in publications or collections; they were then properly attributed.

The Collections

During the immediate postwar period, many governments felt it their duty to remember the concentration camp victims. There was also an organization made up of former camp prisoners whose aim was to preserve the camps as memorials, including museums and shrines. As a result there are major monuments located all over Europe, including the Eastern bloc countries. Many are built on the former camp sites using existing buildings as part of the memorial—the crematoria, the gas chambers, the barracks, the headquarters; and where the camps were liquidated, new structures have been built, often with impressive statuary. Many of the memorials have museums that show all kinds of artifacts from the meagre possessions of the prisoners: eye glasses, bowls, spoons, and clothing, as well as documents, art works, and crafts. In some situations contests were held by various groups to find an "appropriate memorial." In 1953, for example, the Auschwitz Memorial Committee was formed to find such a design. Four hundred and twenty-six designs by 600 artists were submitted to a jury of selection chaired by the noted Henry Moore. One of the stipulations of the contest was, ironically, "artists who once collaborated with the executioners should not take part." Many controversies developed, and Moore felt the submissions had not yet the impact, attitude, or feeling required in such a work to do justice to the prisoners. He resigned, stating: "Only a great sculptor—a new Michelangelo, a new Rodin, could cope with such a task." It was sometime later that a new committee selected a design created by a group of artists and architects who collaborated on the project.[9] This is one memorial that has a museum. At least 500 drawings and paintings are in the collection, about 100 pieces of sculpture and handcrafts. The works of Targosz, Gawron, Gottliebova, Gutkiewicz, Koscielniak, Szajna, Ruzamski, Lieberman, Jazwieki, and others are here. More works by former prisoners done after the liberation are also included today in the museum collection.[10]

In Poland a group of museums, including the one at Auschwitz, held a combined exhibit in 1976 in order "to show the public a part of the collection of paintings, drawings, sculptures, and crafts." The first such exhibit held in Poland, other museums participating in this venture were: the Museum of the Pawiak Prison in Warsaw, which contributed such crafts as an embroidered tablecloth and tassel by Janina Kowalska done in 1940-1941; the Museum of Martyrology and Struggle of Prisoners of War in Lambinowice, where the Lambsdorf prison had been, among the contributions of which was an intricately carved lampshade made from plywood by an unknown prisoner[11]; the State Museum of Maidanek, the death camp in Lublin, which sent as part of its exhibit the sculpture of a tortoise, the symbol of the resistance, carved in concrete by Albin Bo-niecki between 1941 and 1944 while he was imprisoned in Maida-nek; and the State Museum of Stutthof Concentration Camp, located in Sztutowo.[12]

The Jewish Historical Institute in Warsaw has paintings, sculptures, graphics, and metal works by Jewish artists — among them the works by Roman Kramsztyk and Sara Gliksman-Faitlovitz that were salvaged from the Warsaw Ghetto. Opening on April 19, 1971, this institute held an exhibit of 230 paintings, 30 sculptures, and a number of works in metal done by artists in the camps and ghettos.[13]

Intact is Fort Breendonk in Belgium, which the authorities left as it was, from the torture cells to the signs put up by the Nazis. They allowed a change only to make room for a section to house the collection of art works done by the prisoners incarcerated there.[14] Other memorials that also have museums are Sachsenhausen, the former concentration camp near Berlin, and Dachau Concentration Camp near Munich, which was entirely rebuilt in accord with the camp layout. Three chapels have been erected at Dachau by the Jewish, Protestant, and Catholic denominations as shrines to the victims.[15]

The former camp of Mauthausen in Austria has been preserved in its entirety. "A place of warning and commemoration" — the buildings that remained have been left as they were. The "New Hospital," in use by July 1944, accommodates the museum of memorabilia, documents, artworks, crafts, photographs, and other artifacts that were done or owned by the prisoners in the camps. The former laundry now houses a chapel and a meditation room on its upper floor. Some of the buildings have been reconstructed and new commemorative structures in the form of monuments, sculpture, steles and walls have been added to the Mauthausen landscape. At the front main gate to the camp are impressive memorials of the nations: Czechoslovakia, Russia, Luxemburg, Spain, France, Albania, and Poland on one side; and Britain, Belgium, Italy, Hungary, and Yugoslavia on the other side. Further down the road leading to the quarry, *Wiener Graben*, stands the memorial built by the German government and on the site of the old hospital stands the memorial from Austria. At the crematorium in Gusen, former French, Italian, and Belgian prisoners have erected their own monument.[16]

Clandestine artwork was done here and much of it is in the museum or in possession of former prisoners who have given the works to the museum, or donated it on permanent or partial loan. The diversity of the prisoners in nationality and training is evident, but the accounts, like those from all the other camps, about the suffering and atrocities remain the same. Some works are color drawings, like the portrait of Capri di Rimini, a professor of graphic arts from Milan, done by an unknown artist, as well as the drawings by Ludwig Surokowski.[17] A few works, mainly greeting cards, were done in watercolor. Many of the drawings are black and white, like the works of the artist-prisoners: Hans Marsalek, Prüll, Hans Becker, Manuel Alfonso, and M. Billon, an artist from Paris.[18] Another French artist, Bernard Alhebert, completed forty-one works here by April 1944, which are strong graphic portrayals of life in Gusen and Mauthausen.[19] Thirty-two "primitive" drawings by Ludwig Surokowski reveal his experiences in the camp from the moment of his arrest to his liberation.[20] Photographic documents are here as well as photographs of art works done in this camp that are currently owned by others. Among these are photographs of a portrait of Capri di Rimini by the Italian artist, Odiono Ermio,[21] and a group of photographs of powerful drawings by the Russian artist-prisoner, S. Podoroschinj.[22] There are numerous illustrations for various publications done by the camp's artists. Some are caricatures for clandestine newsletters such as the work of Kurt Pany for a Czech newsletter[23] and Ludwik Kopriva who did illustrations for the clandestine periodical, *Hlas Revoluce* ("Voices of the Revolution").[24] Many hand-painted or hand-drawn greeting cards for all occasions — holidays, birthdays, congratulatory — were often inscribed by the artists themselves or by writers in the camps who collaborated with the artists. A poem written by Josef Hora is handwritten and entitled, "Hans der Geigenspieler." A small "booklet" of poems by Zdenk Sekal illustrated with drawings by an unknown Polish artist-prisoner was bound illegally by a Czech bookbinder, and then hidden for months in a tin chest and buried under the barrack entrance of Block 20.[25]

Buchenwald Concentration Camp near Weimar had an active program in the arts, perhaps second only to Terezin. The assignments were done for "the pleasure and profit of the SS," but much secret work was produced and even musical productions took place here. An extensive collection of crafts, art works, music scores, and writings has been preserved and is in this unusual camp collection. Among the craftwork created here are: a pendant carved out of dried beefbone, a clay-modeled lampshade, small carved wooden boxes with lids, pipes, and bookends. A number of sculptures, mainly small wooden carvings like those done in Auschwitz, have been found and are preserved. Many hand-painted and hand-written greeting cards and decorated programs for theater and musical events are also on exhibit. Because of the numerous programs and illustrated music scores that have been saved, it is possible to get an idea of the involvement in the arts in Buchenwald Camp. For example, among the exhibits is a "Konzert Programme" dated 1944, Buchenwald, for a performance of *Don Juan*. There are many hand-written music scores, some of which are embellished with drawings. The music score, *Buchenwalder Lagerlied*, is illustrated in pastel and watercolor. *Arbeitslied* has notes of both clefs clearly written without a musical staff but at the bottom of the score is a drawing of prisoners singing. Another score, *Kopf Hoch*, states that the music was written by Josef Kopinski with words by Bruno Apitz. A songbook, *Liederbuch Buchenwaldsangen*, is also preserved here. Besides illustrating programs and scores, the artists also drew the musicians and musical activities in the camp. A small watercolor called "Probe Im Auditorium Klo," done in 1944 by Karol Konieczny, shows a combo of musicians playing the trumpet, clarinet, and French horn. Another watercolor indicates there was a "camp choir": "Campchoir Of Czech Comrades," by Vladimir Matesjka in 1942. A drawing, "Block Konzert," by Pierre Mania, 1944, shows an accordionist in a central ring surrounded by downcast prisoners. In the catalog of the International Exhibition held in Buchenwald commemorating thirty years of liberation is written: "Never was a song sung giving inspiration and new strength and courage to resist the torture and punishment as those often secretly and softly hummed melodies of the captives in the loneliness of their cells."[26]

Among the secret art works in the Buchenwald Museum's collection done by the prisoners between 1941 and 1945 are fine drawings by Leon Delarbre, Karol Konieczny, Pierre Mania, Henri Pieck, Boris Taslitzky, Vladimir Matesjka, Herbert Sandberg, Tibor Jankai, and an important portrait in pencil of the Terezin artist, Otto Ungar, by Roman Jefimenko, which must have been done shortly before Ungar's death in Buchenwald, Weimar. Small figures carved out of wood and limestone were done by Bruno Apitz and Arthur Birkner during their imprisonment.

The large collection of works at the Terezin Memorial is beautifully arranged, and the exhibit of art works is displayed with professional artistry and sensitivity in the former SS headquarters. The archives are among the best and most expertly cared for, with all

Bruno Apitz   Pendant, Buchenwald Camp
Beefbone carving, 1 ″ × 1½ ″
Courtesy Buchenwald Memorial Museum

Bruno Apitz   Pen holder and ink well, Buchenwald Camp
Wood carving
Courtesy Buchenwald Memorial Museum

works carefully catalogued and filed with an accompanying card-file system including photographs of the works that correspond to the numbered art works. In this collection are over 400 pieces by Leo Haas, the largest body of works by Petr Kien, as well as works by Otto Ungar, whose family in Brno has possession of most of his works; and those of Bloch, Lonek, Marisova, Buresova, Schalkova, Bucanek, Aussenberg, Ginz, Fritta, Fleischmann, Capek, and others. Expertly maintained are countless music scores, costume designs, stage designs, sculptures, prose, poetry, crafts, and other documents. Housed in the *Kleine Festung* section of the ghetto camp, it is an impressive memorial.

The Prague State Jewish Museum also has a large collection of art works, artifacts, and the sacred religious objects of the Jewish faith and tradition. The largest collection of Fleischmann — over 150 works — is here, as are works by Ungar, Haas, Fritta, Aussenberg, and others. In this museum, too, are the 4,000 or so works — drawings and writings — by the children of Terezin.

In Israel, Yad Vashem has a varied selection in its archives. Among these are the works of Daghani, Haas, Hilda Zadikow, Charlotte Buresova, Levy-Lee, Sara Gliksman-Faitlovitz, and others. At the Ghetto Fighters House in Asherat are numerous works by such artists as Feder, Schalkova, Schweisig, Hofstatter, Olomucki, Lurie, Bogen, Carpi, Karas-Kaufman, and Leon Landau. There are other memorials and museums in Israel that have works from the Holocaust period: the Israel Museum in Jerusalem, which had a large exhibit of works by Otto Freundlich — some borrowed and some from their own collection:[27] the Tel Aviv Museum; the Museum of Printing Art, Tel Aviv; and the Museum of Art in Ein Hod.

Documentation centers throughout Europe, such as the Weimar Library in London, the Centre de Documentation Juive Contemporaine in Paris, which has works by Violette le Coq, the Jood Museum in Amsterdam, Il Centro di Documentazione Ebraica Contemporanea in Milano, and the Vatican Museum in Rome all have some data or works in their archives from the Holocaust period, as do the museums established in some of the former ghetto and camp sites. Already-established museums have provided sections for artists who lived in their communities, such as the Osnabruck Museum in Germany, which owns the bulk of the works by Felix Nussbaum, who was born in Osnabruck. In 1971 this museum also honored Nussbaum with a retrospective exhibit of 117 of his works.[28]

Felix Nussbaum   "Organist" (1943)
Painting, 20″ × 25″
Courtesy Osnabruck Museum

In the United States, an impressive collection of varied works and material that is beautifully documented and maintained is at the Leo Baeck Institute in New York City. In that collection are works by Nussbaum, the twenty-five miniature stamps of Karl Schweisig, a Felsenthal diary, Bertalan Gondor cards, watercolors by Fritz Fabian and others. The YIVO Institute, also in New York City, has twelve fine works by Leo Haas, pencil drawings by Adolf Aussenberg, and a few others. The Jewish Archives in Philadelphia owns the file of Dr. Maximilian Pereles in which some art work is included. Many works are privately owned and scattered throughout the world and some are in the United States. A vast private collection of memorabilia, including a small work signed "Lev [Leo] Haas," is owned by Arnold Shay of Wynnewood (near Philadelphia), who has spent his life since his liberation from the camps collecting these artifacts. Another collector of memorabilia, also a survivor, is Yakov Riz of Philadelphia, whose collection consists mainly of written material. A commission was appointed by President Carter in 1979 to make recommendations for an "appropriate memorial" in commemoration of the Holocaust, to be erected in Washington, D.C. The proposal of the commission of thirty-four was that the memorial should be an ongoing educational center with archives, library, and museum as part of the whole. When that center is built, works from privately owned collections will probably find a home. The spillout and overflow of information, documents, and visual material exists all over the world.[29]

A New Movement

Out of that six-year eternity, from the world of camps and ghettos has come such an enormous amount of artwork that it must be considered part of the art of the twentieth century. Enough of it has been salvaged and survived both the ravages of man and nature that it is indeed a veritable art movement, inadvertent though it was. These works fill that hiatus during the war years when the productivity of the major artists of Europe was at an all-time low. Works that are in parts of collections in archives, museums, and private possession all over the world now number over ten thousand.

As difficult as it is to describe or explain anything in regard to the Holocaust era, it must still be remembered that it was and is a part of the history of our times and an event that occurred in the ambience of one of the most cultured societies of the world. It cannot be isolated as an incident that took place in a vacuum. It did not happen in limbo or in hell, it happened on earth. It is woven into the fiber of our history. This we cannot overlook or ignore. The artwork done in this period and under these conditions is a part of the record of this period, not an entity set apart from it. It is a part of the art of our time and must have its berth in the annals of art history of the twentieth century.

The art from the Holocaust, however, cannot be evaluated in ordinary terms. Consideration for all that goes into a work of art alone is inapplicable. The standard measures have to be dispensed with in regard to the art of the found materials and immediate statement, and replaced with another pertinent basis. It is an art that called into play every force of the artist's skill and expertise. It is the art of the caught moment, iced into shape on the eve of a new era by artists cast in the role of chronicler and sufferer. There has to be a new gauge for this art, that was born in conditions such as no artist ever had to endure before. The art must be considered in the context of the Holocaust, and cannot be evaluated without the knowledge of this tragedy and the core from which it emerged.

List of Artists

Enrico Accatino
Mikos Adler
Manuel Alfonso
Bernard Alhebert
Bernard Altschuler
Bruno Apitz
Mier Appelbaum
George Arber
Louis Asher
Edith Auerbach
Adolf Aussenberg
Azriel Awret
Irene Awret

Yehuda Bacon
M. Bahelfer
Schmuel Bak
Jan Bartelman
Bora Baruch
Henoch Barzynsky
Hans Becher
H. Beck
Sali Becker
Henry Behr
Itzak D 'fer
Avram Berline
Elie Berg
L. Berstein-Synayeff
M. Billon
Arthur Birkner
Meijer Bliekrode
Felix Bloch
Alexander Bogen
Albin Boniecki
David Brainin
Jerzy A. Brandhuber
Izak Brauner
Leo Breuer
Aat Breur
Slavko Bril
Alois Bucanek
Jan Budding
Charlotte Buresova
Bzszaszinska

Josef Capek
Aldo Carpi
A. Carvalho
Izak Celniker
Yehuda Cohen
Jacques Cybrynovitch
Samuel Cygler
Branislaw Czech

Arnold Daghani
Mozes Deen
Leon Delarbre
Jessurun Di Mesquita
Capri Di Rimini
Xawrey Dunikowski

Peter Edel
Jonathon Edelson
Maksumilian Elijowicz
Stefana Eljowicz
Henry Epstein
Erno Erb
Odiono Ermio
Emmy Ettinger

165

Fritz Fabian
Joseph Fackeson
Etienne Farcas
Alexander Fasini
August Favier
Aizik Feder
Liesel Felsenthal-Baznitski
Karel Fleischmann
Jindrich Flusser
Marianne Franken
Otto Freundlich
Feliks Friedman
Bedrich Fritta
Jurek Fuks
Feliks Futerman

Salomon Garf
Wincenty Gawron
Peter Ginz
Jacob Glasner
Sara Gliksman-Faitlovitz
Bertalan Gondor
Jules Gordon
Josef Gosschalk
Jacques Gotko
Dinah Gottliebova-Babbitt
Samuel Granowska
Elie Grinnman
K. Guterman
Stanislaw Gutkiewicz

Leo Haas
Mykas Haneman
Robert Hanf
Herta Hausman
Abraham Herman
Adam Herszaft
Abram Hipser
Ignacy Hirszfang
Maria Hiszpanska-Neuman
Osias Hofstatter
Alice Hoherman
Selma Hurwitz

Izkovitch

Jakobsen
Tibor Jankai
Franciszek Jazwiecki
Roman Jefimenko
Judkomski

Danilus Kabiljo
Alfred Kantor
Karas-Kaufman
Jiri Karlinsky
George Kars
Petr Kien
Isis Kischka
Shlomo Klein
Uri Kochba
Moishe Kogan
Herbert Kolb
Karol Konieczny
Ludwig Kopriva
Gertrude Koref
Natan Korzan
Mieczyslaw Koscielniak
Dvora Kowalczyk
Janina Kowalska
J. Kowner
Natalie Kraemer
Roman Kramsztyk
Izak Kreczanowski

David Labkovski
Z. Lachov
Leon Landau
Natalie Landau
Lazar (Mabull)
Tadeusz Lech
Violette Le Coq
Israel Lejzerowicz
Herbert Lender
David Levkovski
Arturo Levy
Robert Levy
Levy-Lee
Ella Lieberman Shiber
George Lielezinski
Jaacov Lifschitz
Lea Lilienblum
Pola Lindenfeld
Riza Liveman
Bohumil Lonek
Loewenhardt
Peter Loewenstein
Joseph Lubitch
Agnes Lukacs
Esther Lurie

Jacob Macznik
T. Manger
Pierre Mania
Hans Marsalek
Vladimar Matesjka
Ota Matousek
Leah Mechalson
L. Mefgashilski
Ephraim Mendalbaum
Abraham Mendelson
Ro Mogendorf
Abrama Mordkhine
Moritz Mueller
Müller
Regina Mundlak
Axel Munk-Anderson
Zoran Music

Moritz Nagel
Arturo Nathan
Abraham Neuham
Felix Nussbaum

Hans Oberlander
Jacques Ochs
David Olere
Halina Olomucki
Daniel Ozono

Abel Pan
Kurt Pany
Bella Pardis
Izak Perel
Henri Pieck
Leonard Pinkhof
Walter Pinto
S. Podoroschinj
Prüll

Rebus
Alexander Reimer
Franciszek Reiz
Joseph Richter
Rilik-Audrieux
Nahum Rombeck
Ozyasz Rosanietsky
Fiszl Rubinlicht
Franka Rubinlicht
M. Ruzamski

Vladimir Sagal
Charlotte Salomon
Herbert Sandburg
Rudolf Saudek
Malvina Schalkova
Savily Schleifer
Schloll
Benzion Josef Schmidt
Raphael Schwartz
Samuel Schwartz
Karl Schweisig
Amalie Seckbach
Faival Segal
Efraim Seidenbeutal
Menasche Seidenbeutal
Gela Seksztein
Kapel Simelewicz
Bruno Simon
Siwek
Marceli Slodki
Jo Spier
Nathan Spigel
Walter Spitzer
M. Staniawska
Zophia Stephen-Bator
Mihajlo Stern
Karel Stipl
Anton Suchecki
Ludwig Surokowski
Jan De Swarte
Igo Sym
Jozef Szajna
Rachel Szalit-Marcus
Jakob Szer
Szymon Szerman
Amos Szwarc
H. Szylis

Franciszek Targosz
Boris Taslitsky
Tolkaczac
Janina Tollik
Simha Trachter
Maurycy Trembacz
Norbert Troller
Leo Turalski
Chaim Tyber
Rachmiel Tynowicki

Peter Ullman
Otto Ungar
Chaim Urrison
Zalman Utkes

Hendrik Valk
Max Van Dam
Marinus Van Raalte
Andre Verlon

Wichinski
Abraham Weinbaum
Ossip Weinberg
Joachim Weingart
Leon Weissberg
Helga Weissova-Hoskova
Simon Wiesenthal
Franciszek Wiezorkowski
Erna Wolfson

Arnold Zadikow
Helena Zadikow
Madim Zardinsky
Fishal Zber
Frantisek Zelenka
Zelniker
Molly Zimetbaum

Notes

Unless otherwise indicated, all the statements of the artists quoted have been taken from interviews recorded on tape and conducted in the language most natural to the artist. Although many artists were multilingual, not all of them spoke English. My conversations with Halina Olomucki were in French, the common language between us. When I had difficulty, the gracious Esther Lurie, who speaks seven languages, translated for me. My entire interview with Sara Gliksman-Faitlovitz was conducted in Hebrew, which I do not speak. Mr. Faitlovitz and Esther Lurie interpreted here. My conversations with Leo Haas were in German and a little English; Reinhard Strecker patiently interpreted our several days of conversation. Zoran Music and I conversed in Italian. At his request, I translated some of his writings which he sent me, as literally and as close to the Italian form as I could. My contact with Dinah Gottliebova-Babbitt, Charlotte Buresova, and Helga Hoskova was mainly by letter.

All other sources and materials used in the preparation of this book are as follows:

■ Artworks, documents, exhibition catalogues, and articles in museums, archives, and documentation centers in the United States, Europe, and Israel, as well as in private collections.

■ Statements, letters, and accounts by the artist-survivors, a former member of the Judenrat, a partisan fighter in the Jewish Brigade, and the soldiers in the liberation forces of the American army.

■ Diaries of prisoners, Sonderkommandos, and Nazis.

My main historical sources were:

Lucy Dawidowicz, *War Against the Jews* (New York: Holt, Rinehart and Winston, 1975).

169

Raul Hilberg, *Destruction of the European Jews* (New York: Quadrangle, 1961).

Nora Levin, *Holocaust: The Destruction of European Jewry, 1939–1945* (New York: Crowell, 1968).

Gerald Reitlinger, *The Final Solution* (Cranbury, N.J.: A.S. Barnes, 1961).

William I. Shirer, *The Rise and Fall of the Third Reich* (New York: Simon & Schuster, 1960).

PREFACE

1. The works of Karl Schweisig were given to the Leo Baeck Institute by Gerhard Mitchell, Castle Cove, Australia, 1972, LBJ News.
2. Nora Levin, "A Plea to Christians," paper delivered at the Second Conference on the Holocaust in Philadelphia, 1976; Gerd Korman, *Silence in the American Text Books* (Jerusalem: Yad Vashem, 1970).
3. Adenauer favored a policy of absorbing minor and repentant Nazis into the mainstream of German Life. James McGovern, *Martin Borman* (New York: Morrow, 1968); Simon Wiesenthal, *The Murderers among Us* (New York: McGraw-Hill, 1976).
4. Reinhard Strecker, *Dr. Hans Globke* (Hamburg: Rutten, Loening Verlag, 1961). Hans Globke, a Nazi, was Adenauer's right-hand man in the government of Germany during his administration. Guido Gerosa, *Il Caso Kappler* (Milan: Sonzogno, 1977).
5. Umberto Giovane's article appeared in *La Parola del Poppolo*, Anno 71, Chicago (November–December, 1979).
6. Lucia Di Riccio, "A Brusar In Risiera," in ibid.; Ferruccio Foelkel, *La Risiera Di San Sabba*, (Verona, Italy: Mondadori, 1979).
7. Gratz College is a Hebrew Educational Institution in Philadelphia.
8. We took twenty-eight rolls of film and recorded ten tapes of interviews and conversations with the artist-survivors.

CHAPTER ONE

1. *Auschwitz, 1940–1945*, guide book (Auschwitz-Birkenau: State Museum in Oswiecim-Brzenzinka, 1978), p. 62.
2. Photographs taken by army sergeant Joseph M. Stellag, 1st Armored Division, 423 F.A. Ballalion, Bty. "B" with General Patton's Third Army in Dachau during the liberation of that camp; Dr. Marcus Smith, *Dachau: The Harrowing of Hell* (Albuquerque: University of New Mexico Press, 1972). An excellent book (with illustrations of Dachau by Zoran Music) written by a doctor in the medical unit of the liberation forces.
3. Nora Levin, "Life Over Death," *Congress Bi-Weekly* 40 (May 18, 1973).
4. Avraham Golub-Tory, "A Paintress in the Ghetto" (biography of Esther Lurie), mimeographed (Tel Aviv, Israel).
5. Leon Delarbre, *Croquis Clandestines*, (Paris: Michel Romilly, 1945), in the YIVO archives, New York.
6. Dr. Burton Wasserman, *Exploring the Visual Arts*, (Worcester, Mass.: Davis Publications, 1976), p. 12.

7. Kenneth Clark, "The Blot and the Diagram," *Encounter* (January 1963), p. 36.

8. Israel Museum Catalog, *Hommage à Otto Freundlich*, 100th Anniversary, No. 183 (September–October 1978), statement by Freundlich, 1936.

9. Ben Shahn, *Biography of a Painting*, (New York: Paragraphic Books, 1966).

10. Sir Herbert Read, *The Meaning of Art* (Baltimore: Penguin, 1931), p. 197.

11. Sabatino Rudio (Sam, Simon, Rudilo), an Italian immigrant-laborer who alone built the awesome Watts Towers out of concrete, faience tile, and crushed glass. Ridiculed during their construction, they are now considered cultural monuments at 107 St., Watts, Los Angeles, California.

12. "B1b" means "Bauabschnitt 1," sector in the process of building. The letter "b" denotes one part of this sector. "Oswiecim W Tworczosci Artystczne," *Katalog Malarstwa* (1962), p. xxxii.

13. Barry Schwartz, *The New Humanism* (New York: Praeger, 1974), pp. 17, 23, 162; Ralph Shikes, *The Indignant Eye* (Boston: Beacon Press, 1969), p. xxvii; "Humanistic Art," in *Encyclopedia of the Arts*, ed. Dagobert D. Runes and Harry Shrickel (New York: Philosphical Library, 1946); John Canaday, *Mainstreams of Modern Art* (New York: Holt, Rinehart and Winston, 1965).

14. Henry Moore, *Sculpture of Henry Moore* (New York: Simon & Schuster, 1968).

15. Kathe Kollwitz, *Diary and Letters of Kathe Kollwitz* ed. Hans Kollwitz (Chicago: Henry Regnery, 1955).

16. "The Charnel House" by Picasso is about the Holocaust tragedy. Picasso remained in Paris during the occupation and was harassed and threatened because his work was considered "decadent art," along with the other avantgarde artists of the time. He was not permitted to exhibit but maintained his studio, which was under constant surveillance. One day an official saw Picasso's sketches for "Guernica" and asked the artist if he did this. Picasso replied, "No, you did."

17. Collection of Mr. and Mrs. Ben Goldstein

18. Jane Biberman, "Survivors," *Inside,* magazine of *Philadelphia Jewish Exponent 1*, 111 (Fall 1980).

19. Correspondence with Olly Ritterband, August 30, 1977.

20. Elsa Pollack, *Auschwitz 5170* (Israel: Ghettos Fighter's House, 1979). An exhibit of her sculpture was held at the Biet Lohamei Haghetaot during the summer of 1979. As I moved around the room filled with her totem-pole figures and gaunt human forms, I felt as if I were in a holy tomb.

21. Itzak Belfer, *The Holocaust* (Tel Aviv: United Artist Ltd, 1971). Janus Korczak was a doctor, educator, and philanthropist who ran an orphanage for the Jewish children in Warsaw. A beloved and respected human being whose real name was Hersh Goldszmit, he considered Polish his mother tongue and used Korczak as his pen name. When the children of his home were taken away to the extermination camps in the Nazi *Aktion*, he chose to go with them although he was told he did not have to go. Much has been written about this great human being as he himself led the children to the *Umschlagplatz* to board the death train.

22. Jacob Landau, famous American artist, quoted in Barry Schwartz, "Tiger of Wrath," *Art in Society 8*, 1 (1977).

23. Lael Wettenbaker, *The World of Picasso* (New York: Time-Life Books, 1971).

24. Poem reprinted by permission of Dr. Miroslav Jaros of the Prague State Jewish Museum.

CHAPTER TWO

1. Jurgen Pieplow, "Kunst und Kunstler in Auschwitz," *Zeichen* (West Berlin), no. 4 (December 1979), p. 10; Dr. Sybil Milton, "Concentration Camp Art and Artists" an excellent article delivered at the Annual Scholars Conference, New York City, 1978; Wolfgang Schneider, *Kunst Hinter Stacheldraft* (Leipzig: Seeman Verlag, 1976).

2. Mauthausen Memorial Museum Catalog, *August 8, 1938–May 5, 1945*, Mauthausen, Austria.

3. Sachsenhausen was established in 1936 and originally set up for political prisoners. It eventually became the espionage center of the SS, and the elite training camp for experimental methods for other camps. An inaccurate estimate of 200,000 prisoners were registered here. (Numbers of those who perished by gassing or shooting were reissued to succeeding prisoners.) Of that number it is believed that 110,000 perished.

4. Gideon Hausner, *Justice in Jerusalem* (New York: Harper & Row, 1966), p. 268.

5. Madelaine Duke, *The Borman Receipt* (New York: Stein & Day, 1978), p. 199.

6. Another account of the abuse of this fake currency is that of a Turk who worked for the British ambassador in Ankara. He sold the plans for Yalta to one of the Nazi attachés at the German embassy. He was paid off with this counterfeit money and years later he tried to sue the Federal Republic of Germany for the money which he claimed was due him.

7. Wiesenthal, *Murderers among Us*; David Roxan and Ken Wanstall, *The Rape of Art* (New York: Coward-McCann, 1964); Matila Simon, *The Battle of the Louvre* (New York: Hawthorn Books, 1971).

8. McGovern, *Martin Borman*; Simon, *Battle of the Louvre*, chap. 3; Roxan and Wanstall, *Rape of Art*, chap. 1.

9. Roxan and Wanstall, *Rape of Art*, chap. 1; Eugene Davidson, *The Trial of the Germans, Nuremburg, 1945–1946* (New York: Macmillan, 1966), p. 90.

10. Silvano Arieti, *The Parnas* (New York: Basic Books, 1975), chap. 10; *Wiesenthal, Murderers among Us*; Duke, *The Borman Receipt*, pp. 75–83. When the war was over many works had to be returned to their rightful institutions because of the careful documents kept by these organizations about the work. The Jewish owners and private citizens whose homes had been ransacked and destroyed have not been so fortunate. How many looted works have really been returned, as claimed by Germany and Austria, to their rightful owners? As recently as 1978 even those who have given minute and detailed descriptions in the Viennese courts of their "one" work or several works have been unable to retrieve what was theirs. Proof of ownership is asked by these courts. How can any of the Jews show proof of ownership when everything they had was destroyed along with their families? Even the great Simon Wiesenthal has intervened in one case at the Monument office, the *Bundesdekmalamt*, that manages the Hofburg in Vienna, where some of the art treasures are stashed away. The government has promised to enact a law, called *Kunstgut-Bereinigungsgesetz*, for the disposition of the art treasures. This was in 1969. But Madelaine Duke, author of *The Borman Receipt*, has been unable to retrieve her property: the Canaletti painting, a work by Reynolds, a painting by Botticelli, and a Vermeyen. According to her book and letters, restitution proceedings drag on, draining the victims financially and psychologically.

According to Simon Wiesenthal, two of Rosenberg's staff are now successful art dealers in the south of Germany, and one of the highest-ranking officials in the Austrian *Bundesdenkmalamt* was one of the SS stormtroopers of the stealing brigade ransacking the museums for the fuhrer.

It is my feeling that there is no doubt that these art works belonged to Jews, and that when the statute of limitations for claims runs out, real justice would dictate that, rather than becoming property of the state of Austria or Germany, these works go to the museums in Israel.

11. Tel Aviv Museum Catalog, Memorial Exhibition, *Jewish Artists Who Perished in the Holocaust*, April–May 1968.

12. Pieplow, "Kunst und Kunstler," pp. 10-11.

13. Ibid.

14. Letter from Henry Swiebocki, Museum Curator, Auschwitz Memorial Museum, Poland, November 30, 1979.

15. "Die Zigeuner-Portraits von Dinah Gottliebova," *Zeichen*, no. 4 (December 1979).

16. Pieplow, "Kunst und Kunstler."

17. Tel Aviv Museum Catalog, *Jewish Artists Who Perished*.

18. Wiesenthal, *Murderers among Us*, pp. 29-32.

19. Ravensbruck bears the stigma of being the camp where medical atrocities performed on women killed them outright or crippled them for life. It was established in 1939 as the only camp for women in the Third Reich. Initially it contained the "opponents" of the Nazi regime in Germany, and later women from other camps began arriving in large numbers. A total of about 132,000 women were incarcerated there, and the deplorable conditions and persecution of the prisoner-women of all nationalities are in all the histories of the Holocaust. Much has been written about the experiments of women referred to as "lapins," and attested to in her own testimony at the Nuremberg Doctor's Trial by Dr. Herta Oberhauser, one of the women doctors who participated in some of the experiments. Norman Cousins did extensive research on what happened to those "lapins" who survived, and was instrumental in helping many get medical treatment and care.

20. Rudolf Hoess, *Autobiography of Hoess (in Auschwitz) 1940–1943*, from *Kl Auschwitz Seen by the SS*, 2nd ed. Panstowe Museum, (Oswiecim, Poland: 1978), pp. 75, 161; Stanislaw Jankowski, deposition, in *Amidst a Nightmare of Crime* (Auschwitz: State Museum, 1973), p. 44; Pery Broad, *Reminiscences of Broad, Kl Auschwitz seen by the SS*, p. 142 fn.

21. Johann Kremer, *Diary of Kremer, Kl Auschwitz Seen by the SS*, pp. 214, 219, 220, and fn. This is an account by one of the doctors who performed experiments on the women in Block 10, which he called *the anus mundi*.

22. This must not be construed to imply in any way that the children were treated well. The extreme brutal treatment and butchery of the little children is the saddest and most inexplicable aspect of the Holocaust. 1,500,000 children were killed by the Nazis. See: Rudolf Hoess' own account in his *Autobiography*, pp. 97-100, 103; Thomas Geve, "Youth in Chains," *Jerusalem Post*, Israel, 1958; Elie Wiesel, *Night* (New York: Avon Books, 1969).

23. Freddi Hirsh was the camp leader of a group who had come from Terezin believing the lie that they were under quarantine in the isolated section of Birkenau camp. He was told that his people were really marked for "special treatment" (in Nazi word-juggling this meant extermination in the gas chambers). Finding out the truth and fearing the inhuman massacre of the children in his charge, he killed himself with veronal on March 7, 1944 — the day the quarantine expired — and all the Czech Jews, including the children, were gassed. Nora Levin, *Holocaust: The Destruction of European Jewry, 1939–1945* (New York: Crowell, 1968), p. 189.

24. Levin, *Holocaust*.

25. Yad Vashem Archives, Jerusalem, Israel, June 1979.

26. Hoess, *Autobiography*.

27. Mauthausen, near Linz, Austria (Hitler's home town), was purposefully located at the quarry site, *Wiener Graben*, so that slave labor could be fully used. Mauthausen, the "mother camp," was an enormous complex with forty-nine satellite camps, including Ebensee, where the prisoners had constructed tunnels leading to an underground oil refinery; Gusen, which housed the armaments factories and brickworks and where artwork was done; Hinterbruhl, the center for the manufacturing and construction of aircraft; Schloss-Mittersill, called the "women's research institute"; Castle Hartheim, used for euthanasia before the war, and one of several extermination centers for the prisoners; and Schlier, where the "forgery commando" tried to set up shop.

28. Letter from Simon Wiesenthal: "Concerning the drawings of the coffee house for my comrade in Mauthausen, I don't have any copies of them," June 18, 1980, Vienna, Austria.

29. Wiesenthal, *Murderers among Us*, p. 31.

30. Alwin Meyer, "Ein Mensch Bleiben der Maler Jerzy Adam Brandhuber," *Zeichen*, no. 4 (December 1979).

31. Hoess, *Autobiography*.

32. Ibid.

33. Cracow was the city in Poland where that country's strongest *avant-garde* movement in the arts was founded, as early as 1897. This group was known as the *Sztuka* (Art). Interested in new trends, they reacted against the historical art of the nineteenth century, introduced new, simple motifs, and revived folklore in art. Many had been chosen to represent Poland in important exhibitions and some had exhibited in the official Polish *Zachenta* (National Institution for the Promotion of Plastic Arts).

34. Pieplow, "Kunst und Kunstler".

CHAPTER THREE

1. Alexander Bogen, *Revolt* (Jerusalem: Yad Vashem, 1974).

2. Alwin Meyer, "Ich Kam Durch, Der Maler Jozef Szajna," *Zeichen,* no. 4 (December 1979).

3. Thomas A. Idinopulos, "Art and the Inhuman: A Reflection on the Holocaust," paper for the Second Conference on the Holocaust, Philadelphia, 1977.

4. Interview with Mr. Tory in Tel Aviv, June 1979.

5. Esther Lurie, *Jewess in Slavery* (Rome: Jewish Soldiers Club, 1945).

6. Alfred Kantor, *The Notebook of Alfred Kantor* (New York: McGraw-Hill, 1971).

7. Vatican Archives, interview with Dr. Mario Ferazzi, director of the contemporary collection of the Vatican museum; Aldo Carpi, *Il Diario di Gusen* (Milan: Garzanti Editore, 1973), diary entry of Wednesday, May 2, 1945.

8. M. Costanza, *The Living Witness Catalog,* Holocaust Conference in Philadelphia, 1978; Letter from M. Meinz, director of Osnabruck Museum.

9. Many letters that are in the Freundlich archives were written on behalf of Otto Freundlich by his friends: Paul Signac, Picasso, Piet Mondrian, and a special letter, "Un appel en Faveur de Otto Freundlich," sent on July 10, 1938, and signed by the above as well as Arp, Braque, Derain, Ernst, Gropius, Kandinsky, Jacob, the historian Herbert Read, and others; Israel Museum Catalog, *Hommage à Otto Freundlich*.

10. Maidanek Death Camp in Poland (*Konzentrationslager Lublin*), established in the autumn of 1941, was originally a prisoner-of-war camp. The first prisoners were German criminals, but later in 1942 transports with Jews of Slovakia, Poland, Greece, and the General Government were sent here. First installation put into action for the extermination of the prisoners with Zyklon B was in May and June 1942. The total number of persons killed at Maidanek amounted to over 360,000.

11. Jasenovac Death Camp, in Levin, *Holocaust,* pp. 514, 515.

12. Terezin Catalog, *Archives of the Terezin Memorial Museum,* Petr Kien, Catalog, Pamatnik, Terezin, 1971; Hubert Saal, "Death Takes a Holiday," *Newsweek* (1977).

13. Yad Vashem Archives, Jerusalem; Terezin Catalog; Catalog, *First Exhibit of Paintings from Camps and Ghettos* (May 5, 1959, Nisan 27th, 5719), Jerusalem.

14. Hausner, *Justice in Jerusalem,* p. 192.

15. Dr. E. van Voolen, Joods Historisch Museum, Amsterdam, Holland, September 4, 1979 (letter).

16. Tel Aviv Museum Catalog, *Jewish Artists Who Perished;* Cecil Roth, *Jewish Art* (rev. Greenwich, Conn.: Graphic Soc. Ltd., 1971), pp. 234-235.

17. Milton, "Concentration Camp Art and Artists."

18. Lawrence Langer, *The Art of the Concentration Camps, Sh'ma 8,* no. 159 (September 29, 1978).

19. Ibid.

20. Antonina Vallentin, *Leonardo da Vinci* (New York: Viking Press, 1938), pp. 404-405.

CHAPTER FOUR

1. Ferdinand Gregorovious, *The Ghettos and Jews of Rome* (New York: Schocken Books, 1948).

2. Earl A. Schleunes, *The Twisted Road to Auschwitz, 1933-1939* (Chicago: University of Illinois Press, 1970); Levin, *Holocaust.* Forced immigration of the wealthier Jews was lucrative for the SS, who confiscated all the properties and possessions of these Jews. Many accounts describe the looting of silver, paintings, and tapestries. Baron de Rothschild was able to emigrate by selling his steel mills to Hermann Goering. In Vienna, approximately 18,000 Jews were forced to buy their way out. Those who couldn't pay were compelled to be "helped" by those who were financially capable. "The rich had to provide for the poor," according to Eichmann.

3. Levin, *Holocaust*; Hausner, *Justice in Jerusalem*; Leonard Tushnet, *The Uses of Adversity* (New York and London: A.S. Barnes, 1966), chaps. 1-3.

4. Lurie, *Jewesses in Slavery.*

5. Jacob Robinson, *The Holocaust, The Catastrophe of European Jews* (Jerusalem: Yad Vashem, 1976), p. 247.

6. Isaiah Trunk, *Judenrat,* (New York: Macmillan, 1972).

7. Ibid.

8. "Art in the Concentration Camps and Ghettoes," in *Encyclopedia Judaica,* vol. 3 (Jerusalem: Keter Publishing House Ltd., 1971), pp. 567-574.

9. Trunk, *Judenrat.*

10. Ibid., pp 196-215. Because of the insistence of teachers, educators, and other adults, there were amazingly fine educational instructions given in some of the ghettos to the children and young adults. This too depended largely on the

size and condition of the ghetto, and on timing. During September 1941 in the Warsaw Ghetto up to 10,000 children were enrolled in makeshift schools and taught by fine teachers. There were children's clubs, educational clubs, young adult organizations, and vocational training. For those children who had to work in such places as the work brigades, factories, or with the "resistance," special lessons were arranged whenever possible.

Extensive educational programs were conducted in the ghettos of Vilna, Lodz, Cracow, Radom, Marysin, and others. In Lodz, in March 1940, around 10,500 children were registered in the elementary schools, and 500 in the high school. There were also courses offered on the college level, in vocational training, and in farming. In Vilna, "the teachers and children carried away the rubble and the rocks and bricks out of the ruins . . . and cleared the way for a classroom. There were no benches and the children sat on dirt floors" (Trunk, *Judenrat*). There were no books, but 2,100 children were in school the first year. Some ghettos, such as Zamocs, Lyczyca, and Lwow, did not permit schooling. Others started but were forced to close. Everything was as see-saw as was typical of the Nazi rationale that could liquidate a whole area at the writing of a single directive.

11. Ibid., pp. 225–227.
12. Ibid., p. 371, ill.
13. Leonard Tushnet, *The Pavement to Hell* (New York: St. Martin's Press, 1972), p. 36.
14. Trunk, *Judenrat*.
15. Tel Aviv Museum Catalog, *Jewish Artists Who Perished*.
16. Roth, *Jewish Art*.
17. Emmanuel Ringelblum, *Notes from the Warsaw Ghetto* (New York: Schocken Books, 1974).
18. Tel Aviv Museum Catalog, *Jewish Artists Who Perished*.
19. Trunk, *Judenrat*.
20. Avraham Golub Tory, *"Biography of Benzion Yosef Schmidt,"* mimeographed (Tel Aviv, Israel).
21. Tel Aviv Museum Catalog, *Jewish Artists Who Perished*.
22. Vilna Album Committee, *Jerusalem of Lithuania* (Egg Harbor City, N.J.: Laureate Press, 1974), reproductions, pp. 460–468.
23. Tel Aviv Museum Catalog, *Jewish Artists Who Perished*.
24. Mordecai Gebertig was the writer of many Yiddish poems and songs that have been set to music and are becoming increasingly well known among Jewish scholars and other interested people.
25. Gerhard Schoenberger, *The Yellow Star* (New York: Bantam Books, 1979).
26. Trunk, *Judenrat*.
27. Ringelblum, *Notes from the Warsaw Ghetto*.
28. Letter from Charlotte Buresova, Prague, Czechoslovakia, May 19, 1980.

CHAPTER FIVE

1. Vice Reichsprotektor, SS Obergruppenfuhrer, Reinhard Heydrich, extract of an official document, October 10, 1941, Prague Castle, Czechoslovakia.
2. Ibid., October 17, 1941.
3. Council of Jewish Community in Czech Lands, *Terezin* (Prague: The Council, 1965), p. 23.
4. Letter from Alfred Kantor.

5. Levin *Holocaust,* Council of Jewish Community in Czech Lands, *Terezin;* Dr. Livia Rothkirchen, *"Czech Attitudes Towards the Jews"* (reprint), *Yad Vasem Studies* 17 (1979).
6. Council of Jewish Community in Czech Lands, *Terezin.*
7. Deputy member of the Council of Elders in Terezin.
8. This cell was large enough for one very small cot and, at that, it was claustrophobic. It was big enough for two or three prisoners at most.
9. Excerpt from conversation with Leo Haas, June 1979, in Berlin.

CHAPTER SIX

1. The twin brother artists, Efraim and Menasche Seidenbeutal of Warsaw, were killed in Flossenburg Camp in April 1945, a few days before the liberation of that camp. The painter of Jewish themes, Jacob Montchink, died in Mauthausen on the eve of the liberation. Arturo Nathan of Trieste was found by the Allies too late to save him from dying of starvation when Bergen-Belsen was freed. Otto Ungar died in a Weimar hospital a few days after he was liberated from Buchenwald.
2. Hans Helmut Janse, *Der Tod in Dictung, Philosophie, Und Kunst* (Darmstadt, Germany: Steinkopff, 1978), p. 148.
3. Ibid.
4. Exhibit catalog, Terezin, *Petr Kien,* 1971. I saw the large collection of Kien's works in Terezin which were done on a variety of surfaces.
5. The Schloll watercolor is in the collection of the Jewish archives in Philadelphia in the Dr. Maximillian Perelez file. Ferramonti di Tarsia was the camp located about twenty-six miles south of Naples near Cosenza.
6. Writings about artists' materials and proper methods for their implementation go back to ancient Greece, to authors such as Vitruvius and Pliny. Cennino Cennini, a student of Giotto, in the thirteenth century wrote "A Treatise on Painting," which is full of "good advice" about materials and other things. Giotto made his own brushes and favored white boar's bristles over the black. Michelangelo dug up his own red and yellow ochres from the clay behind the Vatican for his frescoes in the Sistine Chapel.

Modern technology does not require that the artists make their own materials. Yet it is vital that artists know the science of the materials they use. Many works by today's masters are already in a state of disrepair and deterioration owing to indifference or lack of knowledge about the handling and composition of materials.
7. Pieplow, "Kunst und Kunstler."
8. Terezin Catalog, *Archives of the Terezin Memorial Museum;* Israel Museum Catalog, *Hommage à Otto Freundlich.*
9. Terezin archives and accounts related by Dr. George Maleninsky and chief archivist Jaroslava Bezdekova.
10. Kazimierz Smolen, *In Memory of a Human Tragedy* (Warsaw: Wydawnictivo Katalogow-Cennikow, 1976).
11. Primo Levi, *Se Questo e un Uomo,* ed. Giulio Einaudo (Turin: S.P.A., 1959); trans., *Survival in Auschwitz* (New York: Macmillan, 1961).

CHAPTER SEVEN

1. Salmen Gradowski, in *Amidst a Nightmare of Crime,* pp. 71, 76.
2. Auschwitz—1940–1945, guidebook, pp. 89, 90; "Photo of Objects," p. 88.

3. Lurie, *Jewesses in Slavery.*

4. Meyer, "Ich Kam Durch."

5. Conversation with Miriam Novitch, May 1978.

6. Kantor, *Notebook.*

7. Pieplow, "Kunst und Kunstler," p. 11.

8. Ibid.

9. Letter from Swiebocki, Auschwitz Memorial Museum.

10. Hausner, *Justice in Jerusalem,* p. 322.

11. Fort Breendonk is an old fort, situated halfway between Brussels and Antwerp in Flanders and dating back to World War I, which the Gestapo took over and made into a "reception camp." Every type of torture was practiced here. Unlike many camps that have been either entirely reconstructed as memorials, or refurbished and "cleaned up," the curators of the Belgian National Museum have left everything as it was in the years 1941 to 1944, even the yellowed signs on the wall, "Those Found Past This Point Will Be Shot." The fortress-camp also has a museum section that houses, among other things, the art works done in the prison. The works of the painter Jacques Ochs, who was born in Nice but lived in Liège, Belgium, and was incarcerated here, are in the collection.

12. Esther Lurie, *A Living Witness* (Tel Aviv: Dvir Publishing, 1958).

13. Manuscripts in Yiddish of an unknown Sonderkommando, in *Amidst a Nightmare of Crime,* pp. 111, 122.

14. Miriam Novitch, *Resistenza Spirituale 1940–1945* (Milan: Commune di Milano, 1979).

15. Ringelblum, *Notes from the Warsaw Ghetto,* p. xxi. The carefully hidden archives were found deep under the ruins of the Warsaw Ghetto. The first section was located in September 1946 in boxes; the second section was found sealed in a rubberized milk can in December 1951.

16. The Terezin archives.

17. Yad Vashem Catalog, *First Exhibit of Paintings;* Tel Aviv Museum Catalog, *Jewish Artists Who Perished.*

18. Smith, *Dachau: The Harrowing of Hell.*

19. Letter from Dr. Edwin A. Smolin, Medic, Liberation Forces, Dachau.

20. Letter from Alfred Kantor.

21. Miriam Novitch, "Mai Nessuno nelle stesse condizioni" (No one ever under the same conditions), *Comune di Milano,* July 1979.

22. Manuscripts of Sonderkommando Salmen Leventhal, in *Amidst a Nightmare of Crime,* p. 127.

23. Broad, *Reminiscences.*

CHAPTER EIGHT

1. Levin, *Holocaust,* p. 117.

2. In America vast amounts of World War II data are stored in the National Archives (the Defense Intelligence Agency, custodian of World War II aerial reconnaissance records, has its records stored in a computer; Library of Congress, Washington, D.C.; War Records Center in Alexandria, Va.; U.S. Army, Historical Division: Documentary Section, Pueblo Army Depot. Dino Brugioni and Robert G. Poirer, in *Holocaust Revisited* (monograph prepared for National Archives) describe important findings by the two CIA analysts, which show the kinds of material preserved in these archives.

3. Conversation with Avraham Tory.

4. Smith, *Dachau: The Harrowing of Hell*; letter from Dr. Edward Smolin.

5. Tel Aviv Museum Catalog, *Jewish Artists Who Perished.*

6. Leo Baeck Institute Archives, New York.

7. Aussenberg drawing in collection of the YIVO Institute in New York.

8. "Art in the Concentration Camps," *L.B.I. News* 39, (Winter 1980), p. 7.

9. Adolph Reith, *Monuments to the Victims of Tyranny* (New York: Praeger, 1969).

10. Auschwitz Memorial Museum Catalog, *In Memory of a Human Tragedy,* 1976.

11. Lambsdorf Prison was really a prisoner-of-war camp for Russian and British soldiers.

12. Auschwitz Catalog, *In Memory of a Human Tragedy.*

13. *Biuletyn,* Jewish Historical Institute, Warsaw, no. 4/80 (1971).

14. Letter (September 29, 1980) from Paul M.G. Levy, professor and president of Fort Breendonk, which was made a national memorial in 1947. A public institution supported by the government, its collection consists of drawings by Jacques Ochs, ordered by the SS to draw a gallery of his prisoners; drawings by an artist named Melis; and graffiti on the walls in the cells for solitary confinement.

15. Reith, *Monuments.*

16. Mauthausen Memorial Museum Catalog, *August 8, 1938–May 5, 1945.*

17. Photographs and data from the Atalier-Fuhrherr, Vienna.

18. Ibid.

19. Works listed in notes 21 to 25 below are on loan to the Mauthausen Museum.

20. Dr. Jan Tarasiewicz, Poland.

21. Sokol (architect), Brussels.

22. Donated to the Museum by the Soviet Committee for Veterans, Moscow.

23. Possession of K. Pany, Prague.

24. Possession of Marsalek, Vienna.

25. Possession of Marsalek, Vienna.

26. Wolfgang Schneider, *Lebenswille Hinter Stacheldraht,* Exhibition Catalog, International exhibit (Buchenwald, 1975).

27. Israel Museum Catalog, *Hommage à Otto Freundlich.*

28. Letter from Dr. M. Meinz, museum direktor, Kulturgeschichlices Museum, Osnabruck.

29. In their report to President Carter, the commission, led by author Elie Weisel, recommended, among other things, that the building for the memorial be a part of a federal institution, perhaps the Smithsonian.

Index

A

Albania, 156
Aldoubi, Zvi, 16
Alfonso, Manuel, 157
Alhebert, Bernard, 157
America, 16, 151. *See also* United
    States
American, 23, 24, 144
Apitz, Bruno, 158
Archives, 24, 101, 104, 141, 158,
    162, 174n, 178n
Archivist, 16, 18, 36, 61
    Kaplan, C., 141
    Ringelblum, E., 141
    Tory, A., 98, 139
Armenians, 64
Art
    abstract, 6, 8
    assigned art, 16, 21–48, 93–95,
        117, 146, 162–163
    for barter, 42–43
    children's, 74–77
clandestine art (secret), 16,
    52–86, 95–102, 146,
    156–158
collecting, 25
decadent art (degenerate), 24,
    34, 65, 67, 131, 171n
definition of, 2, 6, 10, 74, 86
design, 2, 6
diversity of, 64–71
exploitation of, 13, 93
of the ghetto, 92–102
humanistic, 1, 6–8, 10, 53,
    79–86
materials, 46, 117–132
message, 6, 8, 10
movement, 10, 64, 65, 101,
    162–163
recovery of, 141–147
of the resistance, 48, 79
robbery, 24, 172, 173n
shops, 13, 23 (*see also* Studios)
smuggling of, 117, 137, 139
Artifacts, 154–156, 160–162

181

ᚻ

I

ℵ

O